CIA
TARGETS
FIDEL

CIA
TARGETS
FIDEL

**SECRET 1967
CIA INSPECTOR GENERAL'S
REPORT ON PLOTS
TO ASSASSINATE FIDEL CASTRO**

Ocean Press
www.oceanbooks.com.au

ISBN 978-1-875284-90-0

First Printed 1996
Reprinted 2003, 2018

Printed in Colombia by Editorial Nomos S.A.

PUBLISHED BY OCEAN PRESS

PO Box 1015, North Melbourne, Victoria 3051, Australia
E-mail: info@oceanbooks.com.au

OCEAN PRESS TRADE DISTRIBUTORS

United States: **Consortium Book Sales and Distribution**
Tel: 1-800-283 3572   www.cbsd.com

Canada: **Publishers Group Canada**
Tel: 1-800-663 5714   E-mail: customerservice@raincoast.com

Australia and New Zealand: **Ocean Press**
E-mail: orders@oceanbooks.com.au

UK and Europe: **Turnaround Publisher Services**
Tel: (44) 020-8829 3000   E-mail: orders@turnaround-uk.com

Cuba and Latin America: **Ocean Sur**
E-mail: info@oceansur.com

ocean

www.oceanbooks.com.au
info@oceanbooks.com.au

Publisher's note

This previously secret CIA report is reprinted as it was declassified in 1994. It has been retyped from the original document. All spelling, punctuation, annotation and underlining are as in the original. The deletions are blacked-out as they are in the document. These deletions remain to be declassified by the CIA. All "Comments" interspersed throughout the document are those prepared by the report's CIA authors.

Preceding the 1967 report by the CIA Inspector General is an interview with Division General Fabián Escalante, former head of Cuba's counterintelligence body. Escalante is Cuba's foremost authority on CIA covert operations against Cuba and the attempts to assassinate Fidel Castro.

Background to CIA assassination plots against Fidel Castro

Interview with Division General Fabián Escalante, former head of Cuban State Security

I have read the report by the CIA Inspector General on the attempts to assassinate Fidel Castro, a report written in 1967 and declassified only recently. I must confess that when I first picked up the report, I did so with some scepticism, since I expected a rather dry document. But two aspects of the report immediately caught my attention: its fascinating subject matter and its style, for it read very much like a spy novel. However, far from fiction, it portrays a crude reality.

The coldness with which the report admits that criminal plans had been drawn up against the president of a neighboring country — Cuba — and that other assassination attempts had been made in different parts of the world also gripped me. The fact that the report was made at the request of Richard Helms, then Director of the Central Intelligence Agency (who had been named to that post less than a year earlier), showed that he had no documentary proof of "undercover actions" in his files — which the report admits. This gave him plenty of room for using the defense of "plausible denial." In fact, Helms continued those assassination plots right up to his replacement in February 1973.

The authors unblushingly admit not only to assassination attempts, but also to the use of the Mafia (bluntly referred to as "hoodlums" or "thugs") and Cuban counterrevolutionaries, in close coordination with U.S. government officials.

This "secret — eyes only" document has now been published 27 years after its writing. Originally prepared in response to probing by U.S. journalist Drew Pearson about the assassination schemes, the report notes that in his March 7, 1967, column Pearson "refers to a reported CIA plan in 1963 to assassinate Cuba's Fidel Castro. Pearson also has information, as yet unpublished, to the effect that there was a meeting at the State Department at which assassination of Castro was discussed and that a team actually landed in Cuba with pills to be used in an assassination attempt. There is basis in fact for each of those three reports."

The report also admits that on November 22, 1963, Rolando Cubela, CIA agent AM/LASH, was given a pen-syringe to be used in assassinating Castro: "It is likely that at the very moment President Kennedy was shot a CIA officer was meeting with a [CIA] Cuban agent in Paris and giving him an assassination device for use against Castro."

Because of this and other information in the report, I decided to seek the comments of a prominent member of Cuban State Security who had recently released some secret information from Cuban files concerning the links between the plans to assassinate Fidel Castro and the plot that finally, using the mechanisms created under Operation ZR/RIFLE, ended the life of President Kennedy.

Division General Fabián Escalante Font was a member of the Cuban Ministry of Interior unit that countered the CIA's schemes; later on he headed the Cuban Department of State Security. At present, he is delving more deeply into these matters and working on a book on the main assassination attempts against Fidel Castro, based on Cuban State Security secret documents.

Though starting to gray at the temples, Escalante is still a young man. Tall, thin and with a rather mysterious or reserved manner, as well befits a spy chief, he has an extraordinary memory for facts, names and dates — undoubtedly developed in his years of evaluating reports from widely dispersed sources that had to be put together like a jigsaw puzzle to find out what the enemy to the north was really up to. Far from being a cold personality, when moved he speaks with great passion about each of the many operations in which he has taken part.

The dialogue which follows took place in a house in Havana on a suffocatingly hot morning.

✪

Question: Both the investigations of the U.S. Senate in 1975 and the recently declassified report of the CIA Inspector General recognize that there were eight plots to assassinate Fidel Castro, but most of them, according to the investigators, were never implemented. Would you like to comment on this?

Escalante: The U.S. Senate Committee that investigated the assassination attempts against Fidel Castro in 1975 examined those activities that unexpectedly began to be exposed in the late 1960s. In 1966 and 1967, the U.S. press published some reports about the mafioso John Rosselli, saying that he had worked to overthrow the Cuban government by trying to assassinate Fidel Castro at the beginning of that decade. Another of the plots that was made public to some extent was the AM/LASH case involving Rolando Cubela Secades, who had been a commander in the Rebel Army and who was arrested in Cuba in 1966 for his participation in plans to assassinate Fidel. His trial brought out his close ties to the U.S. Central Intelligence Agency. It should be kept in mind that it was this same agent, Rolando Cubela, who was given a pen on November 22, 1963 — the day on which John Kennedy was assassinated — for use in killing Fidel Castro.

This coincidence led U.S. investigators to query why, at precisely the same time President Kennedy was assassinated, the

CIA was giving one of its men, agent AM/LASH, an object to be used in another assassination — the plot against Fidel Castro. Thus, by the mid-1960s two main plots against Fidel Castro had been exposed — the Mafia plan later dubbed the poison pill plot and the CIA plot involving Cubela (AM/LASH) — as well as an earlier CIA plan to assassinate Fidel during his visit to the UN in September 1960. On that occasion, a CIA officer proposed to a U.S. police captain who headed Fidel's bodyguard that he kill the Cuban leader with an explosive cigar. Those were the three main plots that were known at that time.

Other schemes were devised later on, such as poisoning a diving suit, placing an explosive shell on the beach, putting chemical substances in a cigar which would cause temporary confusion and spraying LSD in a television studio that would give Fidel an attack of uncontrollable laughter. Another plan that was attempted in New York in 1960 involved putting thallium salts in Fidel's shoes to make his beard fall out — the beard was thought to be the key to his charismatic appeal as a legendary guerrilla.

It should be noted that these plots were made public as the result of the fallout from the Watergate scandal and the increasingly discredited image of the CIA. In fact, the U.S. Senate investigations in 1975 made no more than a superficial analysis of the CIA's attempts to assassinate Fidel Castro. If you read with close attention the Senate report and this one by the Inspector General, you will see that they tried to make readers believe that many of these plans were either not implemented at all or were aborted part way along. This was not so, as we can demonstrate.

That is, they weren't just abstract plans but were supposed to be implemented — or, at least attempts were to made to implement them.

Yes, such attempts were made. Many of these plans reached the implementation stage; Cuban Security units countered some of them, and others failed by chance or because of planning errors.

The first attempts to assassinate Fidel began prior to the triumph of the revolution. One famous plan in 1958 involved Eutimio Rojas, a traitor whom Batista's army bribed to kill Fidel while he slept in his camp in the Sierra Maestra mountains. But when it came to the decisive moment, Rojas chickened out.

A U.S. citizen was supposed to carry out the first assassination attempt that was planned after the 1959 revolution. It was to take place on February 2, 1959, when Allan Robert Nye landed near Havana in a light plane. Nye had made deals with some big names in organized crime — members of the gambling syndicate, which, as you'll remember owned a lot of property in Cuba such as big gambling casinos, big hotels, etc. He was planning to assassinate Fidel Castro near the former Presidential Palace. Armed with a powerful rifle with a telescopic sight, Nye waited at a hotel near the Presidential Palace for Fidel Castro to arrive at his office, which was located in the Palace at that time; he was arrested before he could fire a shot.

The following month, on March 26, 1959, Rolando Masferrer Rojas, the former head of one of Batista's death squads, who was then in the United States and in contact with the CIA, suggested another plot for assassinating Fidel, also near the Presidential Palace. Both the CIA and the gambling syndicate in Havana gave it their OK.

The most salient aspect of all the assassination plots against Fidel Castro following the triumph of the revolution in 1959 was the high degree of support they had in the CIA and the complicity of the U.S. government.

Two things bear this out. The first is that in early December 1959, Colonel J.C. King, head of the Western Hemisphere Division of the CIA, sent a memo to his chief, Allen Dulles, in which he stated that they would have to do away with Fidel Castro if they wanted to overthrow the Cuban revolution. He recommended this course of action officially. That report is part of the declassified material that appeared in the U.S. Senate's 1975 investigation. It

marked the beginning of the legal framework for the CIA's plans
to assassinate Fidel. That memo was written by the head of the
Western Hemisphere Division, and Allen Dulles, Director of the
CIA, approved it.

The second thing showing the complicity in such plans of the
CIA and the U.S. government was the role of the U.S. embassy in
Havana. Cuban Security was working on a very important case,
which we called the Opera Case. U.S.-Cuban relations hadn't
yet been broken off. The United States had a strong embassy
presence. Phillip Bonsal was ambassador and James Noel was
head of the CIA station. Around 20 CIA operatives worked there,
including Major Robert Van Horn, one of the military attaches.
Van Horn was linked to a counter-revolutionary organization
that was being formed in Havana and Miami, called the Anti-
Communist Workers' Militia (MAO). A CIA agent called Geraldine
Shapman headed the organization which was connected to several
counterrevolutionary groups in Miami, including that of Rolando
Masferrer Rojas. In December 1959, this group proposed to CIA
officer Robert Van Horn that Fidel Castro be assassinated while
visiting the Miramar home of Commander Ramiro Valdés — that
an ambush be set there for this purpose. This plan was considered
and sent on to the CIA for a decision and Lois C. Herber, a U.S.
citizen who was in charge of Central America and the Carribean in
the CIA, visited our country in January and February 1960 to meet
with the plotters and see how the plan was coming along.

In that period, we had two agents in the CIA center in
the embassy: Comrade Luis Tacornal, known as Fausto, and
José Veiga Peña, now a lieutenant colonel in the Ministry of
the Interior. They met with both Van Horn and Herber and
formed part of the commando group that was to carry out the
assassination attempt. We were faced with the dilemma of what
to do. If Fidel stopped going to Commander Ramiro Valdés' house
the conspirators might become suspicious, and we wanted the
operation to last long enough to enable us to learn what the CIA's
plans were. Therefore our agents proposed to the CIA that, until

the right time came for assassinating Fidel, they should first try to assassinate Commander Abelardo Colomé Ibarra, who was one of the chiefs of G-2 [Cuban State Security Department] at the time and is now Minister of the Interior.

Their proposal was accepted. A plan was drawn up for a shoot-out at the corner of First and B Streets where a skirmish took place in which blanks were used. That made it possible for our agents to take their weapons — which were to have been used in the attempt against Fidel — and "lose" them. Geraldine Shapman's group hid our agents in different places, and the attack on Fidel was put off until November 1960, by which time the members of the group were arrested and their plans denounced.

I've cited this case because it took place at the end of 1959 and early 1960 — after Colonel King presented his memo — and because we have irrefutable proof of the involvement of the U.S. embassy and a CIA officer stationed in Havana who was supervised by a high-ranking CIA chief who came to meet with the plotters (including our agents).

That's why I said that the assassination attempts against Fidel began quite a while before December 1960 (the date given in the 1967 report); in fact, assassination attempts have been made against him for more than 35 years.

The U.S. investigators say, however, that those things happened a long time ago and that the CIA doesn't approve of such practices now. Do you think the CIA still wants to assassinate Fidel?

There's one important thing we should remember. All of the plans to assassinate Commander Fidel Castro have been related and very closely linked to the interests of the United States — and of course, to the CIA's obsession with overthrowing the Cuban revolution, which, as you know, is still very much alive. I could give you a lot of examples in this regard, but I don't want to cite the ones that are mentioned in the Inspector General's report. There is another one, however, that shows how closely the strategy of assassinating

Fidel is linked to overthrowing the Cuban revolution. It was planned for 1962, in the context of Operation Mongoose, which was one of the largest operations the U.S. government has ever mounted against Cuba. It wasn't just a CIA operation but rather had the backing of the entire U.S. government, as a part of which an economic blockade was imposed against our country and the members of the Organization of American States — with the sole, honorable exception of Mexico — were forced to break off their relations with Cuba. Operation Mongoose also involved a plan which we called Operation Botín. It consisted of psychological warfare using subversive radio stations (the same ones that are now broadcasting against Cuba) and printed propaganda. Printed material was dropped on Cuba's coastline in plastic bags with straw inside to make them float; the bags also contained chewing gum. The propaganda called on the people to assassinate Fidel Castro and other Cuban leaders offering a series of "bounties": $150,000 for Fidel Castro, $120,000 for Raúl Castro, $120,000 for Che Guevara and $100,000 for the President of the Republic. A price was listed for every Cuban official. Just imagine: thousands of pieces of propaganda sent to the Cuban people calling on them to assassinate their leaders with specific sums offered in payment! I think that this example shows just how far the CIA was willing to go and how great its effort was to try to assassinate Fidel Castro in those years.

You have said that there were many more than the eight plots listed in the Inspector General's report and that they differed widely, including not only the use of agents but also actively encouraging and inciting people's own initiative, so to speak. That business of including chewing gum was quite ingenious — or, rather, disgraceful. Do you believe that assassination attempts are still being planned?

Yes, of course. In fact, I've just spent a lot of time in the Ministry of the Interior's files doing research on the plots against Fidel over the last 35 years. We have documentation on 612 of them, but I think there were even more, because in the early years, when the Department of State Security was very new, it had little organizational skill. In many cases, when plans were implemented and our Security units frustrated them, they may not have been recorded.

Those 612 plots were in the 1959-93 period. Naturally, not all were of the same quality. Their level of planning wasn't the same. Conditions have changed, in both Cuba and the United States, so they had to be drawn up differently. The processes of planning and carrying out these 612 conspiracies differed from one to another. While it was fairly easy for their perpetrators up through the 1970s — having a base of operations both here and in the United States which helped them to move the men, weapons and money they required — it became much more difficult for them in the 1980s.

We can identify several assassination plans that were drawn up subsequent to the Inspector General's report. For example, the CIA planned for Antonio Veciana's group to assassinate Fidel Castro while he was visiting Chile, Ecuador and Peru in 1971. In 1976 the CIA designed a plot for assassinating Fidel on his departure for Angola to attend the November 11 ceremony inaugurating the first national government to be established in that country. Here I'm talking about two relatively recent attempts. It goes without saying that there were others in the late 1970s and throughout the 1980s. I remember, for example, that the CIA and Cuban counterrevolutionaries in Miami planned to assassinate Fidel when he went to Venezuela to attend the 1989 presidential inauguration there. They failed, both because of the security measures we took and because of assistance from the Venezuelan authorities; moreover, the atmosphere there was such that the would-be assassins couldn't get close to Fidel Castro.

We learned so far ahead of time of other plans that were to be carried out in Cuba that we were able to neutralize them or cause them to be aborted right at the beginning, in the initial planning stage.

Do you think it's important that these documents have been declassified? Previously, Cuba was the only one who was exposing these things. Now that these documents have been declassified, perhaps as a result of pressure which some sectors in the United States have brought to bear, don't you think this backs up what Cuba has been saying for so many years?

Yes I do. It's important that these documents have been declassified, because they show not only that the CIA wanted to assassinate Fidel Castro, but also that the CIA set up a mechanism in early 1961 for assassinating other foreign political leaders who opposed U.S. policy.

I think that many of the political phenomena that have appeared in the United States in the last 35 years have been related to this process — to the CIA's war against Cuba and the mechanisms that were created in that period. I say this because the ZR/RIFLE project was created in January 1961. That project is still in effect, using different names but with the same purpose of assassinating political leaders.

That same project was linked to the death of Orlando Letelier, who was Foreign Minister in Salvador Allende's administration, and to the assassination of General Omar Torrijos, President of Panama. (The Torrijos assassination was linked to Manuel Artime Buesa, a Cuban counterrevolutionary and CIA agent who had been imprisoned in Cuba.) ZR/RIFLE was also involved with many "coincidental" deaths that took place in the United States and the assassination of revolutionary leaders in Latin America — I'm referring to all of the assassinations, including those of political leaders such as Colombian presidential candidate Galan four years ago. It was part of that project because the U.S. intelligence community had accepted and recognized political assassination as a effective tool for applying U.S. policy.

The fact is that the CIA created its largest operational base in the world, with more than 400 case officers and over 4,000 agents (and its only such base in the United States) in Miami in 1962. This base even had planes, a navy and innumerable fronts for concealing its actions. The ultrasecret Operation 40, an anti-Cuba structure of the CIA which was later linked to the Watergate scandal through Frank Sturgis, Eugenio Martínez and others who worked on it, had its headquarters in that large operational base.

I have said before and continue to believe that President Kennedy's assassination was also the work of that same criminal conspiracy, which had been created for use against Cuba before he took office. Thus, it was used not only against Fidel Castro but against other leaders as well — even the President of the United States, John F. Kennedy.

After this dialogue, I found the Inspector General's report to be even more interesting reading. Escalante is now working on a new book on the assassination attempts against Fidel Castro, who remains one of the most hated — and most loved — of world leaders today.

Mirta Muñiz
Havana
September 1994

Translated by Mary Todd

23 May 1967

MEMORANDUM FOR THE RECORD

SUBJECT: Report on Plots to Assassinate Fidel Castro

This report was prepared at the request of the Director of
Central Intelligence. He assigned the task to the Inspector
General on 23 March 1967. The report was delivered to the Director,
personally, in installments, beginning on 24 April 1967. The
Director returned this copy to the Inspector General on 22 May 1967
with instructions that the Inspector General:

    Retain it in personal, EYES ONLY safekeeping

    Destroy the one burn copy retained temporarily by the
    Inspector General

    Destroy all notes and other source materials originated
    by those participating in the writing of the report

The one stayback burn copy, all notes, and all other derived
source materials were destroyed on 23 May 1967.

This ribbon copy is the only text of the report now in existence,
either in whole or in part. Its text has been read only by:

    Richard Helms, Director of Central Intelligence
    J. S. Earman, Inspector General
    K. E. Greer, Inspector (one of the authors)
    S. D. Breckinridge, Inspector (one of the authors)

All typing of drafts and of final text was done by the authors.

Filed with the report are:

    Office of Security file used as source material
    Memorandums concerning William Harvey
    Certain MONGOOSE papers
    Drew Pearson columns

J. S. Earman
Inspector General

Opening page from original 1967 CIA report

10 - 11 August 1962

█████, █████, and Cubela met in Copenhagen for further meetings. █████ wrote in his contact report:

" . . . at one time when we █████ always wrote of himself as 'we'] were discussing the various aspects of Cubela's future role in Cuba, we used the term 'assassinate.' The use of this term, we later learned from █████ and from Cubela himself, was most objectionable to the latter, and he was visibly upset. It was not the act he objected to, but rather merely the choice of the word used to describe it. 'Eliminate was acceptable.'"

(Comment: It is worth noting here that █████ a Cuban █████ in New York, was present at a series of meetings at which the assassination of Castro was discussed between Cubela and █████ whom █████ knew to be a CIA officer.)

14 - 23 August 1962

Cubela, █████ and █████ met in Paris and were joined by █████ a Spanish-speaking case officer █████ Cubela was given S/W training and was issued appropriate S/W supplies. He was taken to the south of France on 20 August for a demolition demonstration. █████ planned to polygraph Cubela and asked for a polygraph operator to be sent to Paris. Cubela indignantly refused to be polygraphed. █████ cabled on 17 August:

"Have no intention give Cubela physical elimination mission as requirement but recognize this something he could or might try to carry out on his own initiative."

Headquarters replied by cable on 18 August:

"Strongly concur that no physical elimination missions be given Cubela."

29 August 1962

Cubela left Prague by air for Havana.

- 85 -

When declassified in 1994, sections of the CIA report were deleted

23 May 1967

MEMORANDUM FOR THE RECORD

SUBJECT: *Report on Plots to Assassinate Fidel Castro*

This report was prepared at the request of the Director of Central Intelligence. He assigned the task to the Inspector General on 23 March 1967. The report was delivered to the Director, personally, in instalments, beginning on 24 April 1967. The Director returned this copy to the Inspector General on 22 May 1967 with instructions that the Inspector General:

> Retain it in personal, EYES ONLY safekeeping

> Destroy the one burn copy retained temporarily by the Inspector General

> Destroy all notes and other source materials originated by those participating in the writing of the report.

The one stayback burn copy, all notes, and all other derived source materials were destroyed on 23 May 1967.

This ribbon copy is the only text of the report now in existence, either in whole or in part. Its text has been read only by:

Richard Helms, Director of Central Intelligence

J.S. Earman, Inspector General

K.E. Greer, Inspector (one of the authors)
S.D. Breckinridge, Inspector (one of the authors)

All typing of drafts and of final text was done by the authors.

Filed with the report are:

Office of Security file used as source material
Memorandums concerning William Harvey
Certain MONGOOSE papers
Drew Pearson columns

J.S. Earman
Inspector General

TABLE OF CONTENTS

Cubela and Juan Orta want to exfiltrate (Mar 61)

Cubela asks for meeting in Paris (Aug 61)

Cubela plans to attend Helsinki Youth Festival

Meetings in Helsinki (Aug 62)

Meetings in Stockholm

Cubela objects to the word "assassinate"

Paris meetings (Aug 62); S/W & demolition training

Meetings in Porto Alegre (Sept 63)

Paris meetings (Oct 63); Cubela wants assurance from U.S. Govt

FitzGerald meets with Cubela in Paris (Oct 63)

Differing versions of what FitzGerald told Cubela

Cuba cache approved for Cubela

The Black Leaf 40 scheme is discussed

Gunn converts a ballpoint pen into a hypodermic syringe

██████ gives to Cubela in Paris while Kennedy is shot

Cubela asks for high-powered rifle with telescopic sight

Those witting of the Black Leaf 40 episode

Cubela cache put down (without rifles) (Mar 64)

Cubela requests a silencer for a FAL rifle

SAS requests TSD to produce FAL silencer on crash basis

Second Cubela cache put down (with FAL rifles)(June 64)

Artime meets Cubela intermediary

Artime agrees to meet with Cubela personally

██████ meets Cubela in Paris (Dec 64)

Explanation of how Artime and Cubela were put together

Artime and Cubela meet in Madrid (Dec 64)

Artime agrees to furnish silencer

Artime gives Cubela silencer and other special gear

Second name-line between Cubela and gambling syndicate operation

Headquarters terminates all contacts with Cubela group

Cubela and others arrested; plead guilty (Mar 66)

The charges

OUTLINE

25 April 1967

MEMORANDUM

This reconstruction of Agency involvement in plans to assassinate Fidel Castro is at best an imperfect history. Because of the extreme sensitivity of the operations being discussed or attempted, as matter of principle no official records were kept of planning, of approvals, or of implementation. The few written records that do exist are either largely tangential to the main events or were put on paper from memory years afterwards. William Harvey has retained skeletal notes of his activities during the years in question, and they are our best source of dates. Dr. Edward Gunn, of the Office of Medical Services, has a record of whom he met and when and cryptic references to the subjects discussed. ████████ of TSD, has a record of two or three dates that are pertinent. Gunn and ████████ were involved in only the technical aspects of operational planning, and their participations were short-lived. Although fragmentary, their records are a help in establishing critical time frames. Operational files are useful in some instances, because they give dates of meetings, the substances of which may be inferred from collateral information.

For the most part, though, we have had to rely on information given to us orally by people whose memories are fogged by time. Their recollection of dates are particularly hazy, and some of them are no longer able to keep the details of one plan separate from those of another. We interviewed everyone whom we could identify as likely to be knowledgeable, with the exceptions of Mr. Dulles and General Cabell. A complete list is attached at Tab A. We did not go on fishing expeditions among the mere possibles. To have done so would have risked making witting a number of employees who were previously unwitting and, in our estimate, would have added little to the details available from those directly involved. There are inconsistencies among the various accounts, but most of them can be resolved by collating the information furnished by all of the identifiable participants in a particular plan and by then checking it against specific dates that can be fixed with fair certainty. We believe that this reconstruction of what happened and of the thinking associated with it is reasonably sound. If there are significant inaccuracies in the report, they are most likely to occur in faulty ordering of the sequence of events. People still remember much of what happened, but they can no longer recall precisely when.

It became clear very early in our investigation that the vigor with which schemes were pursued within the Agency to eliminate Castro personally varied with the intensity of the U.S. Government's efforts to overthrow the Castro regime. We can identify five separate phases in Agency assassination planning, although the transitions from one to the another are not always sharply defined. Each phase is a reflection of the then prevailing Government attitude toward the Cuban regime.

a. Prior to August 1960: All of the identifiable schemes prior to about August 1960, with one possible exception, were aimed only at discrediting Castro personally by influencing his behaviour or by altering his appearance.

b. August 1960 to April 1961: The plots that were hatched in late 1960 and early 1961 were aggressively pursued and were viewed by at least some of the participants as being merely one aspect of the over-all active effort to overthrow the regime that culminated in the Bay of Pigs.

c. <u>April 1961 to late 1961</u>: A major scheme that was begun in August 1960 was called off after the Bay of Pigs and remained dormant for several months, as did most other Agency operational activity related to Cuba.

d. <u>Late 1961 to late 1962</u>: That particular scheme was reactivated in early 1962 and was again pushed vigorously in the era of Project MONGOOSE and in the climate of intense administration pressure on CIA to do something about Castro and his Cuba.

e. <u>Late 1962 until well into 1963</u>: After the Cuban missile crisis of October 1962 and the collapse of Project MONGOOSE, the aggressive scheme that was begun in August 1960 and revived in April 1962 was finally terminated in early 1963. Two other plots were originated in 1963, but both were impracticable and nothing ever came of them.

We cannot overemphasize the extent to which responsible Agency officers felt themselves subject to the Kennedy administration's severe pressures to do something about Castro and his regime. The fruitless and, in retrospect, often unrealistic plotting should be viewed in that light.

Many of those we interviewed stressed two points that are so obvious that recording them here may be superfluous. We believe, though, that they are pertinent to the story. Elimination of the dominant figure in a government, even when loyalties are held to him personally rather than to the government as a body, will not necessarily cause the downfall of the government. This point was stressed with respect to Castro and Cuba in an internal CIA draft paper of October 1961, which was initiated in response to General Maxwell Taylor's desire for a contingency plan. The paper took the position that the demise of Fidel Castro, from whatever cause, would offer little opportunity for the liberation of Cuba from Communist and Soviet Bloc control. The second point, which is more specifically relevant to our investigation, is that bringing about the downfall of a government necessarily requires the removal of its leaders from positions of power, and there is always the risk that the participants will resort to assassination. ~~Such removals from power as the house arrest of a Mossadeq or the flight of a Batista should not cause one to overlook the killings of a Diem or of a Trujillo by forces encouraged but not controlled by the U.S. Government.~~

There is a third point, which was not directly made by any of those we interviewed, but which emerges clearly from the interviews and from review of files. The point is that of frequent resort to synecdoche — the mention of a part when the whole is to be understood, or vice versa. Thus, we encounter repeated references to phrases such as "disposing of Castro," which may be read in the narrow, literal sense of assassinating him, when it is intended that it be read in the broader, figurative sense of dislodging the Castro regime. Reversing the coin, we find people speaking vaguely of "doing something about Castro" when it is clear that what they have specifically in mind is killing him. In a situation wherein those speaking may not have actually meant what they seemed to say or may not have said what they actually meant, they should not be surprised if their oral shorthand is interpreted differently than was intended.

The suggestion was made to us that operations aimed at the assassination of Castro may have been generated in an atmosphere of stress in intelligence publications on the possibility of Castro's demise and on the reordering of the political structure that would follow. We reviewed intelligence publications from 1960 through 1966, including National Intelligence Estimates [NIE], Special National Intelligence Estimates [SNIE], Intelligence Memorandums, and Memorandums for the Director. The NIE's on "The Situations and Prospects in Cuba" for 1960, 1963 and 1964 have brief paragraphs on likely successor governments if Castro were to depart the scene. We also find similar short references in a SNIE of March 1960 and in an Intelligence Memorandum of May 1965. In each case the treatment is no more nor less than one would expect to find in comprehensive round-ups such as these. We conclude that there is no reason to believe that the operators were unduly influenced by the content of intelligence publications.

Drew Pearson's column of 7 March 1967 refers to a reported CIA plan in 1963 to assassinate Cuba's Fidel Castro. Pearson also has information, as yet unpublished, to the effect that there was a meeting at the State Department at which assassination of Castro was discussed and that a team actually landed in Cuba with pills to be used in an assassination attempt. There is basis in fact for each of those three reports.

a. A CIA officer passed an assassination weapon to an Agency Cuba asset at a meeting in Paris on 22 November 1963. The weapon was a ballpoint pen rigged as a hypodermic syringe. The CIA officer suggested that the Cuban asset load the syringe with Black Leaf 40. The evidence indicates that the meeting was under way at the very moment President Kennedy was shot.

b. There was a meeting of the Special Group (Augmented) in Secretary Rusk's conference room on 10 August 1962 at which Secretary McNamara broached the subject of liquidation of Cuban leaders. The discussion resulted in a Project MONGOOSE action memorandum prepared by Edward Lansdale. At another Special Group meeting on 31 July 1964 there was discussion of a recently-disseminated Clandestine Services information report on a Cuban exile plot to assassinate Castro. CIA had refused the exile's request for funds and had no involvement in the plot.

c. CIA twice (first in early 1961 and again in early 1962) supplied lethal pills to U.S. gambling syndicate members working in behalf of CIA on a plot to assassinate Fidel Castro. The 1961 plot aborted and the pills were recovered. Those furnished in April 1962 were passed by the gambling syndicate representative to a Cuban exile leader in Florida, who in turn had them sent to Cuba about May 1962. In June 1962 the exile leader reported that a team of three men had been dispatched to Cuba to recruit for the operation. If the opportunity presented itself, the team would make an attempt on Castro's life — perhaps using the pills.

This report describes these and other episodes in detail; puts them into perspective; and reveals, that while the events described by Drew Pearson did occur and are subject to being patched together as though one complete story, the implication of a direct, causative relationship among them is unfounded.

Miscellaneous Schemes
Prior to August 1960

March to August 1960

We find evidence of at least three, and perhaps four, schemes that were under consideration well before the Bay of Pigs, but we can fix the time frame only speculatively. Those who have some knowledge of the episode guessed at dates ranging from 1959 through 1961. The March-to-August span we have fixed may be too narrow, but it best fits the limited evidence we have.

a. None of those we interviewed who was first assigned to the Cuba task force after the Bay of Pigs knows of any these schemes.

b. J.D. (Jake) Esterline, who was head of the Cuba task force in pre-Bay of Pigs days, is probably the most reliable witness on general timing. He may not have been privy to the precise details of any of the plans, but he seems at least to have known of all of them. He is no longer able to keep the details of one plan separate from those of another, but each of the facets he recalls fits somewhere into one of the schemes. Hence, we conclude that all of these schemes were under consideration while Esterline had direct responsibility for Cuba operations.

c. Esterline himself furnishes the best clue as to the possible time span. He thinks it unlikely that any planning of this sort would have progressed to the point of consideration of means until after U.S. policy concerning Cuba was decided upon about March 1960. By about the end of the third quarter of 1960, the total energies of the task force were concentrated on the main-thrust effort, and there would have been no interest in nor time for pursuing such wills-o'-the-wisp as these.

We are unable to establish even a tentative sequence among the schemes; they may, in fact, have been under consideration simultaneously. We find no evidence that any of these schemes was approved at any level higher than division, if that. We think it most likely that no higher-level approvals were sought, because none of the schemes progressed to the point where approval to launch would have been needed.

Aerosol Attack on Radio Station

███████████ of TSD remembers discussion of a scheme to contaminate the air of the radio studio where Castro broadcast his speeches with an aerosol spray of a chemical that produces reactions similar to those of lysergic acid (LSD). Nothing came of the idea. ███████████ said he had discouraged the scheme, because the chemical could not be relied upon to be effective. ███████████, also of TSD, recalls experimentation with psychic energizers but cannot relate it to Castro as a target. We found no one else who remembered anything of this plot, with the possible exception of Jake Esterline who may have it confused with other schemes.

Contaminated Cigars

Jake Esterline claims to have had in his possession in pre-Bay of Pigs days a box of cigars that had been treated with some sort of chemical. In our first interview with him, his recollection was that the chemical was intended to produce temporary personality disorientation. The thought was to somehow contrive to have Castro smoke one before making a speech and then to make a public spectacle of himself. Esterline distinctly recalls having had the cigars in his personal safe until he left WH/4 and that they definitely were intended for Castro. He does not remember how they came into his possession, but thinks they must have been prepared by ███████. In a second interview with Esterline, we mentioned that we had learned since first speaking with him of a scheme to cause Castro's beard to fall out. He then said that his cigars might have been associated with that plan. Esterline finally said that, although it was evident that he no longer remembered the intended effect of the cigars, he was positive they were not lethal. The cigars were never used, according to Esterline, because WH/4 could not figure out how to deliver them without danger of blowback on the Agency. He says he destroyed them before leaving WH/4 in June 1961.

Sidney Gottlieb of TSD, claims to remember distinctly a plot involving cigars. To emphasize the clarity of his memory, he named the officer, then assigned to WH/CA, who approached him with the scheme. Although there may well have been such a plot, the officer Gottlieb named was then assigned in India and has never worked in WH Division nor had anything to do with Cuba operations. Gottlieb remembers the scheme as being one that was talked about frequently but not widely and as being concerned with killing, not merely with influencing behaviour. As far as Gottlieb knows, this idea never got beyond the talking stage. TSD may have gone ahead and prepared the cigars just in case, but Gottlieb is certain that he did not get the DD/P's (Richard Bissell) personal approval to release them, as would have been done if the operation had gone that far. We are unable to discover whether Esterline and Gottlieb are speaking of a single cigar episode or of two unrelated schemes. We found no one else with firm recollections of lethal cigars being considered prior to August 1960.

Depilatory

███████████ recalls a scheme involving thallium salts, a chemical used by women as a depilatory — the thought being to destroy Castro's image as the "The Beard" by causing the beard to fall out. The chemical may be administered either orally or by absorption through the skin. The right dosage causes depilation; too much produces paralysis. ████████ believes that the idea originated in connection with a trip Castro was to have made outside of Cuba. The idea was to dust thallium power into Castro's shoes when they were put out at night to be shined. The scheme progressed as far as procuring the chemical and testing it on animals. ████████ recollection is that Castro did make the intended trip, and the scheme fell through. ████████ remembers consideration being given to use of thallium salts (perhaps against Castro) and something having to do with boots or shoes. ████████ does not remember with whom he dealt on this plot. We found no one else with firm knowledge of it.

Gambling Syndicate

The first seriously-pursued CIA plan to assassinate Castro had its inception in August 1960. It involved the use of members of the criminal underworld with contacts inside Cuba. The operation had two phases: the first ran from August 1960 until late April or early May 1961, when it was called off following the Bay of Pigs; the second ran from April 1962 until February 1963 and was merely a revival of the first phase which had been inactive since about May 1961.

Gambling Syndicate — Phase 1

August 1960

Richard Bissell, Deputy-Director for Plans, asked Sheffield Edwards, Director of Security, if Edwards could establish contact with the U.S. gambling syndicate that was active in Cuba. The objective clearly was the assassination of Castro although Edwards claims that there was a studied avoidance of the term in his conversation with Bissell. Bissell recalls that the idea originated with J.C. King, then Chief of WH Division, although King now recalls having had only limited knowledge of such a plan and at a much later date — about mid-1962.

Edwards consulted Robert A. Maheu, a private investigator who had done sensitive work for the Agency, to see if Maheu had any underworld contacts. Maheu was once a special agent of the FBI. He opened a private office in Washington in 1956. The late Robert Cunningham, of the Office of Security (and also a former Special Agent with the FBI), knew Maheu and knew that his business was having a shaky start financially. Cunningham arranged to subsidize Maheu to the extent of $500 per month. Within six months Maheu was doing so well financially that he suggested that the retainer be discontinued. Over the years he has been intimately involved in providing support for some of the Agency's more sensitive operations. He has since moved his personal headquarters to Los Angeles but retains a Washington office. A more detailed account of Maheu's background appears in a separate section of this report.

> (Comment: Although we see nothing sinister in it, we are struck by the fact that so many of the persons whose names appear in this account once worked for the FBI. We have already named Cunningham and Maheu. Later to appear are William Harvey, James O'Connell, and Edward Morgan.)

Maheu acknowledged that he had a contact who might furnish access to the criminal underworld, but Maheu was most reluctant to allow himself to be involved in such an assignment. He agreed to participate only after being pressed by Edwards to do so. Maheu identified his contact as one Johnny Roselli, who lived in Los Angeles and had the concession for the ice-making machines on "the strip" in Las Vegas and whom Maheu understood to be a member of the syndicate. Maheu was known to Roselli as a man who had a number of large business organizations as clients. Edwards and Maheu agreed that Maheu would approach Roselli as the representative of businessmen with interests in Cuba who saw the elimination of Castro as the essential first step to the recovery of their investments. Maheu was authorized to tell Roselli that his "clients" were willing to pay $150,000 for Castro's removal.

September 1960
Shef Edwards named as his case officer for the operation James P. O'Connell (a former Special Agent of the FBI), then Chief,

Operational Support Division, Office of Security. O'Connell and Maheu met Roselli in New York City on 14 September 1960 where Maheu made the pitch. Roselli initially was also reluctant to become involved, but finally agreed to introduce Maheu to "Sam Gold" who either had or could arrange contracts with syndicate elements in Cuba who might handle the job. Roselli said he had no interest in being paid for his participation and believed that "Gold" would feel the same way. A memorandum for the record prepared by Sheffield Edwards on 14 May 1962 states: "No monies were ever paid to Roselli and Giancana. Maheu was paid part of his expense money during the periods that he was in Miami." (Giancana is "Gold.")

O'Connell was introduced (in true name) to Roselli as an employee of Maheu, the explanation being that O'Connell would handle the case for Maheu, because Maheu was too busy to work on it full time himself. No one else in the Office of Security was made witting of the operation at this time. Edwards himself did not meet Roselli until the summer of 1962.

At this point, about the second half of September, Shef Edwards told Bissell that he had a friend, a private investigator, who had a contact who in turn had other contacts through whom syndicate elements in Cuba could be reached. These syndicate elements in Cuba would be willing to take on such an operation. As of the latter part of September 1960, Edwards, O'Connell, and Bissell were the only ones in the Agency who knew of a plan against Castro involving U.S. gangster elements. Edwards states that Richard Helms was not informed of the plan, because Cuba was being handled by Bissell at that time.

With Bissell present, Edwards briefed the Director (Allan Dulles) and the DDCI (General Cabell) on the existence of a plan involving members of the syndicate. The discussion was circumspect; Edwards deliberately avoided the use of any "bad words." The descriptive term used was "an intelligence operation." Edwards is quite sure that the DCI and the DDCI clearly understood the nature of the operation he was discussing. He recalls describing the channel as being "from A to B to C." As he then envisioned it, "A" was Maheu, "B" was Roselli, and "C" was the principal in Cuba. Edwards recalls that Mr. Dulles merely nodded, presumably in understanding and approval. Certainly, there was no opposition. Edwards states that, while there was no formal approval as such, he felt that he clearly had tacit approval to use his own judgement. Bissell committed $150,000 for the support of the operation.

(Comment: In the light of this description of the briefing, it is appropriate to conjecture as to just what the Director did approve. It is safe to conclude, given the men participating and the general subject of the meeting, that there was little likelihood of misunderstanding — even though the details were deliberately blurred and the specific intended result was never stated in unmistakable language. It is also reasonable to conclude that the pointed avoidance of "bad words" emphasized to the participants the extreme sensitivity of the operation.)

During the week of 23 September 1960, O'Connell and Maheu went to Miami where Roselli introduced only Maheu to "Sam Gold" at a meeting in the Fontainbleau Hotel. "Gold" said he had a man, whom he identified only as "Joe," who would serve as a courier to Cuba and make arrangements there. Maheu pointed out "Gold" to O'Connell from a distance, but O'Connell never met either "Gold" or "Joe." He did, however, learn their true identities. An Office of Security memorandum to the DDCI of 24 June 1966 places the time as "several weeks later." O'Connell is now uncertain as to whether it was on this first visit to Miami or on a subsequent one that he and Maheu learned the true identities of the two men. Maheu and O'Connell were staying at separate hotels. Maheu phoned O'Connell one Sunday morning and called his attention to the *Parade* supplement in one of that morning's Miami newspapers.

It carried an article on the Cosa Nostra, with pictures of prominent members. The man Maheu and O'Connell knew as "Sam Gold" appeared as Mon Salvatore (Sam) Giancana, a Chicago-based gangster. "Joe, the courier" (who was never identified to either Maheu or O'Connell in any other way) turned out to be Santos Trafficante, the Cosa Nostra chieftain in Cuba.

At that time the gambling casinos were still operating in Cuba, and Trafficante was making regular trips between Miami and Havana on syndicate business. (The casinos were closed and gambling was banned effective 7 January 1959. On 13 January 1959, Castro announced that the casinos would be permitted to reopen for tourists and foreigners but that Cubans would be barred. The cabinet on 17 February 1959 authorized reopening the casino for the tourist trade. *Time* magazine for 2 March 1959 announced that the casinos had been reopened the previous week. The *New York Times* issue of 30 September 1961 announced that the last of the casinos still running had been closed.) Trafficante was to make the arrangements with one of his contacts inside Cuba on one of his trips to Havana.

Fall and Early Winter 1960

Very early in the operation, well before the first contact with Roselli, the machinery for readying the means of assassination was set in motion. The sequence of events is not clear, but it is apparent that a number of methods were considered. Preparation of some materials went ahead without express approval.

(Comment: It should be noted TSD maintains a stock of equipment and materials for operational use. When queries are made of TSD technicians about materials or devices that are not stock items, it is not unusual for the technicians to go ahead with the preparation of the materials or devices against the event that there is a formal request for them. Because of this, undue significance should not be attached to advance preparations for this operation. It should also be noted that it was not unusual at the time in question for the Chief of TSD to be by-passed in operations involving his people. While Cornelius Roosevelt, then Chief of TSD, has the clear impression that all requests were levied through him, instances were cited in the course of this inquiry where such was not the case. The practices and procedures in existence at the time may account, at least in part, for the differing recollections of what did and what did not happen and for the differing degrees of significance given developments in the minds of the participants.)

Dr. Edward Gunn, Chief, Operations Division, Office of Medical Services, has a notation that on 16 August 1960 he received a box of Cuban cigars to be treated with a lethal material. He understood them to be Fidel's favourite brand, and he thinks they were given to him by Shef Edwards. Edwards does not recall the incident. Gunn has a notation that he contacted ■■■■■■■ of TSD, on 6 September 1960. ■■■■■■■ remembers experimenting with some cigars and then treating a full box. He cannot now recall whether he was initially given two boxes, experimenting with one and then treating the other; or whether he bought a box for experimentation, after which he treated the box supplied him by Gunn. He does not, in fact, remember Gunn as the supplier of any cigars. He is positive, though, that he did contaminate a full box of fifty cigars with botulinum toxin, a virulent poison that produces a fatal illness some hours after it is ingested. ■■■■■■■ distinctly remembers the flaps-and-seals job he had to do on the box and on each of the wrapped cigars, both to get at the cigars and to erase the evidence of tampering. He kept one of the experimental cigars and still has it. He retested it during our inquiry and found that the toxins still retained 94% of its original effectiveness. The cigars were so heavily contaminated that merely putting one in the mouth would do the job; the intended victim would not actually have to smoke it.

Gunn's notes show that he reported the cigars as being ready for delivery on 7 October 1960. ■■■■■■'s notes do not show actual delivery until 13 February 1961. They do not indicate to whom delivery was made. Gunn states that he took the cigars, at some unspecified time, and kept them in his personal safe. He remembers destroying them within a month of Shef Edwards' retirement in June 1963.

[In the margin next to the above paragraph a hand-written note reads: "We believe ▮▮▮▮▮▮▮ *gave the cigars to Gunn."]*

(Comment: Others recalls the cigar scheme, but only as an idea that was considered and then discarded. Roosevelt, Chief of TSD at the time, and O'Connell, the case officer, recall the cigar scheme, but feel that it was never considered seriously. To Gunn and ▮▮▮▮▮▮ who gave it a good deal of time but did not participate in the broader operational discussions, the cigars loom as important.)

Edwards recalls approaching Roosevelt after Bissell had already spoken to Roosevelt on the subject; Roosevelt recalls speaking to Edwards after Bissell discussed it with Edwards. Bissell does not recall specific conversations with either of them on the technical aspects of the problem, but he believes that he must have "closed the loop" by talks with both Edwards and Roosevelt. Roosevelt recalls his first meeting with Edwards as being in Edwards' office. Edwards remembers asking to be introduced to a chemist. He is sure that he did not name the target to Roosevelt, but Roosevelt says he knew it was Castro. Roosevelt believes that he would have put Edwards in touch with ▮▮▮▮▮▮▮▮, then chief of TSD's Chemical Division, but ▮▮▮▮▮▮ has no recollection of such work at that time. ▮▮▮▮▮▮ recalls other operations at other times, but not this one. Roosevelt did say that, if he turned it over to ▮▮▮▮▮▮▮ ▮▮▮▮▮▮▮ could have assigned it to ▮▮▮▮▮▮.

Roosevelt remembers that four possible approaches were considered: (1) something highly toxic, such as shellfish poison to be administered with a pin (which Roosevelt said was what was supplied to Gary Powers); (2) bacterial material in liquid form; (3) bacterial treatment of a cigarette or cigar; and (4) a handkerchief treated with bacteria. The decision, to the best of his recollection, was that bacteria in liquid form was the best means. Bissell recalls the same decision, tying it to a recollection that Castro frequently drank tea, coffee, or bouillon, for which a liquid poison would be particularly well suited.

January-February 1961

Despite the decision that a poison in liquid form would be most desirable, what was actually prepared and delivered was a solid in the form of small pills about the size of saccharine tablets. ▬▬▬▬▬ remembers meeting with Edwards and O'Connell in Edwards' office to discuss the requirement. The specifications were that the poison be stable, soluble, safe to handle, undetectable, not immediately acting, and with a firmly predictable end result. Botulin comes nearest to meeting all of those requirements, and it may be put up in either liquid or solid form. ▬▬▬▬▬ states that the pill form was chosen because of ease and safety of handling.

> (Comment: The gangsters may have had some influence on the choice of a means of assassination. O'Connell says that in his very early discussions with the gangsters (or, more precisely, Maheu's discussions with them) consideration was given to possible ways of accomplishing the mission. Apparently the Agency had first thought in terms of a typical, gangland-style killing in which Castro would be gunned down. Giancana was flatly opposed to the use of firearms. He said that no one could be recruited to do the job, because the chance of survival and escape would be negligible. Giancana stated a preference for a lethal pill that could be put into Castro's food or drink. Trafficante ("Joe, the courier") was in touch with a disaffected Cuban official with access to Castro and presumably of a sort that would enable him to surreptitiously poison Castro. The gangsters named their man inside as Juan Orta who was then

Office Chief and Director General of the Office of the Prime Minister (Castro). The gangsters said that Orta had once been in a position to receive kickbacks from the gambling interests, had since lost that source of income, and needed the money.)

When Edwards received the pills he dropped one into a glass of water to test it for solubility and found that it did not even disintegrate, let alone dissolve. ██████ took them back and made up a new batch that met the requirement for solubility. Edwards at that point wanted assurance that the pills were truly lethal. He called on Dr. Gunn to make an independent test of them. Edwards gave Gunn money to buy guinea pigs as test animals. Gunn has a record of a conversation with ██████ on 6 February 1961. It may have related to the tests, but we cannot be sure. What appears to have happened is that Gunn tested the pills on the guinea pigs and found them ineffective. ██████ states that tests of botulin on guinea pigs are not valid, because guinea pigs have a higher resistance to this particular toxin. ██████ himself tested the pills on monkeys and found they did the job expected of them.

We cannot reconstruct with certainty the sequence of events between readying the pills and putting them into the hands of Roselli. Edwards has the impression that he had a favorable report from Dr. Gunn on the guinea pig test. Gunn probably reported only that the pills were effective, and Edwards assumed that the report was based on the results of tests on guinea pigs. Dr. Gunn has a clear recollection, without a date, of being present at a meeting in which Roosevelt demonstrated a pencil designed as a concealment device for delivering the pills. Roosevelt also recalls such a meeting, also without a date. Gunn's notes record that his last action on the operation came on 10 February 1961 when he put Gottlieb in touch with Edwards. Gottlieb has no recollection of being involved, an impression that is supported by Bissell who states that Gottlieb's assignments were of a different nature. O'Connell, who eventually received the pills, recalls that he dealt with ██████. ██████ has no record of delivering pills at this time, but he does not ordinarily keep detailed records of such things.

In any event, O'Connell did receive the pills, and he believes there were six of them. He recalls giving three to Roselli. Presumably the other three were used in testing for solubility and effectiveness. The dates on which O'Connell received the pills and subsequently passed them to Roselli cannot be established. It would have been sometime after Gunn's notation of 10 February 1961.

Gunn also has a record of being approached about the undertaking by William K. Harvey (former special agent of the FBI) in February in connection with a sensitive project Harvey was working on for Bissell. According to Gunn's notes, he briefed Harvey on the operation, and Harvey instructed him to discuss techniques, but not targets, with Gottlieb. Gunn's notation on this point is not in accord with the recollections of any of the others involved. We are unable to clarify it; the note may have been in another context. O'Connell states that J.C. King was also briefed at this time, although King denies learning of the operation until much later.

Late February-March 1961

Roselli passed the pills to Trafficante. Roselli reported to O'Connell that the pills had been delivered to Orta in Cuba. Orta is understood to have kept the pills for a couple of weeks before returning them. According to the gangsters, Orta got cold feet.

(Comment: Orta lost his position in the Prime Minister's Office on 26 January 1961, while planning for the operation was still going on in Miami and in Washington. He took refuge in the Venezuelan Embassy on 11 April 1961 and became the responsibility of the Mexican Embassy when Venezuela broke relations with Cuba in November 1961. Castro refused to give him a safe conduct pass until October 1964 when he was allowed to leave for Mexico City. He arrived in Miami in early February 1965.

(It appears that Edwards and O'Connell did not know at the time of Orta's fall from favor. They have made no reference to it — ascribing Orta's failure to cold feet. It would seem, though, that the gangsters did know that Orta had already lost his access to Castro. They described him as a man who had once had a position that allowed him a rake-off on gambling profits, a position that he had since lost. The only job with which we can associate Orta that might have allowed him a rake-off was the one he held in the Prime Minister's Office, which he lost on 26 January 1961. It seems likely that, while the Agency thought the gangsters had a man in Cuba with easy access to Castro, what they actually had was a man disgruntled at having lost access.)

The previously-mentioned 24 June 1966 summary of the operation prepared by the Office of Security states that when Orta asked out of the assignment he suggested another candidate who made several attempts without success. Neither Edwards nor O'Connell know the identity of Orta's replacement nor any additional details of the reported further attempts.

March-April 1961

Following the collapse of the Orta channel, Roselli told O'Connell that Trafficante knew of a man high up in the Cuban exile movement who might do the job. He identified him as Tony Varona (Dr. Manuel Antonio de VARONA y Loredo). Varona was the head of the Democratic Revolutionary Front, ▄▄▄▄▄▄▄▄▄▄▄▄▄▄▄▄▄▄▄▄▄▄▄▄▄▄▄ part of the larger Cuban operation. O'Connell understood that Varona was dissatisfied ▄▄▄ ▄▄ ▄▄▄▄▄▄▄▄▄▄▄▄▄▄▄▄▄▄▄▄▄▄▄

(Comment: Reports from the FBI suggest how Trafficante may have known of Varona. On 21 December 1960 the Bureau forwarded to the Agency a memorandum reporting that efforts were being made by U.S. racketeers to finance anti-Castro activities in hopes of securing the gambling, prostitution, and dope monopolies in Cuba in the event Castro was overthrown. A later report of 18 January 1961 associates Varona with those schemes. Varona had hired Edward K. Moss, a Washington public relations counselor, as a fund raiser and public relations advisor. The Bureau report alleged that Moss' mistress was one Julia Cellini, whose brothers represented two of the largest gambling casinos in Cuba. The Cellini brothers were believed to be in touch with Varona through Moss and were reported to have offered Varona large sums of money for his operations against Castro, with the understanding that they would receive privileged treatment "in the Cuba of the future." Attempts to verify these reports were unsuccessful.

(There is a record of CIA interest in Moss, but there is no indication that the Agency had any involvement with him in connection with Cuba. ███████████████████████████

██

████████████ In early 1965 Moss became of interest to the House Foreign Affairs Committe because of his record of having represented various foreign governments. A memorandum prepared by CA Staff in March 1965 states that the records do not show any use made of Moss ████████████████████

██

██

██████████████████████

Trafficante approached Varona and told him that he had clients who wanted to do away with Castro and that they would pay big money for the job. Varona is reported to have been very receptive, since it would mean that he would be able to buy his own ships, arms, and communications equipment.

(Comment: By this time Roselli had become certain that O'Connell was an Agency employee, not a subordinate of

Maheu. He told O'Connell that he was sure that O'Connell was "a government man — CIA" but that O'Connell should not confirm this to him. Roselli said that as a loyal American he would do whatever he could and would never divulge the operation.)

Roselli was to deliver money to Varona for expenses. O'Connell now recalls the amount as $50,000. Edwards, who was away at the time, recalls it as $25,000. Since Edwards was absent, O'Connell had to get approval from Edwards' deputy, Robert Bannerman, who until then had been unwitting of the operation. O'Connell told Bannerman that the operation was known to and approved by Edwards. Bannerman authorized passing the money and now recalls the amount as being on the order of $20,000 to $25,000. An Office of Security memorandum to the DDCI, dated 24 June 1966, sets the amount as $10,000 in cash and $1,000 worth of communications equipment. Jake Esterline, who signed the vouchers for the funds, recalls the amounts as being those stated in the Office of Security memorandum.

> (Comment: As a sidelight, Esterline says that, when he learned of the intended use of Varona, steps were taken to cancel the plan. Varona was one of the five key figures in the Revolutionary Front and was heavily involved in support of the approaching Bay of Pigs operation. If steps were in fact taken to end Varona's participation in the syndicate plan, they were ineffective. It is clear that he continued as an integral part of the syndicate scheme.)

When the money was ready, O'Connell took the pills from his safe and delivered them and the money to Roselli. Roselli gave the pills and the money to Varona, whom Roselli dealt with under pseudonym. Little is known of the delivery channels beyond Varona. Varona was believed to have an asset inside Cuba in a position to slip a pill to Castro. Edwards recalls something about a contact who worked in a restaurant frequented by Castro and who was to receive the pills and put them into Castro's food or drink. Edwards believes that the scheme failed because Castro ceased to visit that particular restaurant.

April-May 1961

Soon after the Bay of Pigs, Edwards sent word to Roselli through O'Connell that the operation was off — even if something happened there would be no payoff. Edwards is sure there was a complete standdown after that; the operation was dead and remained so until April 1962. He clearly relates the origins of the operation to the upcoming Bay of Pigs invasion, and its termination to the Bay of Pigs failure. O'Connell agrees that the operation was called off after the Bay of Pigs but that the termination was not firm and final. He believes that there was something going on between April 1961 and April 1962, but he cannot now recall what. He agrees with Bill Harvey that when the operation was revived in April 1962, Harvey took over a "going operation."

> (Comment: As distinguished from Edwards and O'Connell, both Bissell and Esterline place the termination date of the assassination operation as being about six months before the Bay of Pigs. Esterline gives as his reason for so believing the fact that the decision had been made to go ahead with a massive, major operation instead of an individually-targeted one such as this. Whatever the intention in this respect, if the decision to terminate was actually made, the decision was not communicated effectively. It is clear that this plan to assassinate Castro continued in train until sometime after the Bay of Pigs.)

O'Connell believes that he must have recovered the pills, but he has no specific recollection of having done so. He thinks that instead of returning them to TSD he probably would have destroyed them, most likely by flushing them down a toilet. ████ has no record of the pills having been returned to him, but he says he is quite sure that they were.

In a memorandum of 14 May 1962 Sheffield Edwards stated that knowledge of this particular operation was limited to six persons. In the course of this investigation, we have identified the following persons who knew in late 1960 or early 1961 of this specific plan to assassinate Castro:

1. Allen Dulles, Director of Central Intelligence
2. General C. P. Cabell, Deputy Director of Central Intelligence
3. Richard Bissell, Deputy Director for Plans
4. Sheffield Edwards, Director of Security
5. James O'Connell, Office of Security, the case officer
6. J.D. Esterline, Chief, WH/4
7. Cornelius Roosevelt, Chief, TSD
8. ███████ Chemical Division, TSD
9. Edward Gunn, Chief, Operations Division, Medical Services
10. William Harvey, Chief, FI/D
11. Sidney Gottlieb, Special Assistant to the DD/P (Gottlieb's name was encountered repeatedly in this inquiry, but he denies knowing of the operation in 1960-61)
12. Robert Bannerman, Deputy Director of Security
13. J.C. King, Chief, WH Division. (He too denies knowing of the operation at the time.)

The following persons outside the government are known to be witting of the operation and either know or strongly suspect the Agency's connection with it:

1. Robert Maheu, a private investigator
2. John Roselli, the Agency's principal contact with the gambling syndicate

3. Sam Giancana, an important figure in the syndicate

4. Santos Trafficante, the courier and man inside Cuba

These additional people were aware of the operation, but their knowledge of CIA's connection with it can only be speculated:

1. Juan Orta, the man originally selected to poison Castro

2. Antonio Varona, a Cuban exile leader

3. The son-in-law of Varona, who is known to have been involved with him closely during this time. (The Varona 201 file makes no reference to Varona having a son-in-law, but he identified this close associate as such.)

The Agency's General Counsel, Lawrence Houston, and Attorney General Robert Kennedy learned the full details of the operation in May 1962. We do not know the particulars of the report Drew Pearson now has, but it may include many of the details of this operation. If it does, then the circle of those now knowledgeable would be widened to include:

1. Edward P. Morgan, Maheu's Washington attorney

2. Columnist Drew Pearson and probably his partner, Jack Anderson

3. Chief Justice Earl Warren

4. James Rowley, chief of the Secret Service

5. Pat Coyne, Executive Secretary of the PFIAB

6. Attorney General Ramsey Clark

7. Various members of the FBI

Gambling Syndicate — Phase 2

William Harvey, chief of FI/D, was briefed in February 1961 (by authority of Richard Bissell) on phase one of the gambling syndicate operation. That briefing was in connection with a sensitive operation that Bissell had assigned to Harvey. Harvey describes it thus: Early in the Kennedy administration, Bissell called him in to discuss what Harvey refers to as an Executive Action Capability; i.e., a general stand-by capability to carry out assassinations when required. Harvey's notes quote Bissell as saying, "The White House has twice urged me to create such a capability." Bissell recalls discussing the question of developing a general capability with Harvey. He mentioned the Edwards/ gambling syndicate operation against Castro in that context, but he now thinks that the operation was over by then and that reference to it was in terms of a past operation as a case in point. It was on this basis that Harvey arranged to be briefed by Edwards. Harvey's fixing of the date as February was only after review of events both preceding the briefing and following it. He says now that it might have been as early as late January or as late as March 1961.

After some discussion of the problems involved in developing an Executive Action Capability, Bissell placed Harvey in charge of the effort. Harvey says that Bissell had already discussed certain aspects of the problem with ████████ and with Sidney Gottlieb. Since ████ was already cut in, Harvey used him in developing the Executive Action Capability, although never with respect to Castro. We did not question Gottlieb on his knowledge of the program for creating an Executive Action Capability, but Harvey's mention of him in this connection may explain a notation by Dr Gunn that Harvey instructed Gunn to discuss techniques with Gottlieb without associating the discussion with the Castro operation.

Harvey states that after the decision was made to go ahead with the creating of an Executive Action Capability, and while he was still discussing its development with Bissell, he briefed Mr. Helms fully on the general concept but without mention of the then ongoing plan to assassinate Castro.

The Executive Action program came to be known as ZRRIFLE. Its principal asset was an agent, QJWIN, who had been recruited earlier by ▇▇▇▇▇ for use in a special operation in the Congo (the assassination of Patrice Lumumba) to be run by ▇▇▇▇▇ ▇▇▇▇▇ made a survey of the scene, decided he wanted no part in an assassination attempt, and asked to be released — which Bissell granted.) The project name, ZRRIFLE, first appears in the files in May 1961, although the first recorded approval is dated 19 February 1962. The new DD/P (Helms) on that date authorized Harvey, by memorandum, to handle the project on a special basis. Accounting for expenditures was to be by general category and Harvey's certification. The initial approval was for $14,700, consisting of $7,200 for QJWIN's annual salary and $7,500 for operational expenses.

Project ZRRIFLE was covered as an FI/D operation (ostensibly to develop a capability for entering safes and for kidnapping couriers). It continued on a course separate from the Edwards/gambling syndicate operation against Castro until 15 November 1961. Harvey has a note that on that date he discussed with Bissell the application of the ZRRIFLE program to Cuba. Harvey says that Bissell instructed him to take over Edwards' contact with the criminal syndicate and thereafter to run the operation against Castro. Harvey adds that, as a completely unrelated development, shortly after this discussion with Bissell he was told by Helms that he was to be placed in charge of the Agency's Cuba task force.

Late 1961-Early 1962

Harvey recalls that he was very busy with a number of things in the period that followed the discussion with Bissell that led to his taking over Edwards' Castro operation. He was turning over his responsibilities in FI/D. He was working with NSA on the Martin/ Mitchell defection case. He was reading in on Cuba operations and was engaged in daily meetings concerning them. He attended a station chiefs' conference in Panama in late January and early February.

February-March 1962

Harvey recalls a first meeting with Edwards in February 1962 on the subject of the Castro operation. He also recalls working out the details of the takeover during March.

> (Comment: After Harvey took over the Castro operation he ran it as one aspect of ZRRIFLE; however, he personally handled the Castro operation and did not use any of the assets being developed in ZRRIFLE. He says that he soon came to think of the Castro operation and ZRRIFLE as being synonymous. The over-all Executive Action program came to be treated in his mind as being synonymous with QJWIN, the agent working on the over-all program. He says that when he wrote of ZRRIFLE/ QJWIN the reference was to Executive Action Capability; when he used the cryptonym ZRRIFLE alone, he was referring to Castro. He said that his correspondence would disclose this distinction. We reviewed the correspondence and found it for the most part unrevealing.
>
> (After Harvey left Task Force W and was winding up his headquarters responsibilities in preparation for assignment to Rome, he wrote a memorandum to the Chief, FI Staff, dated 27 June 1963, stating that the original justification for employing QJWIN no longer existed and raising the question of QJWIN's termination. The records (■■■-1974, 24 April 1964) show that QJWIN was terminated ■■■■■■■■■■ on the 21 April 1964.

There is no indication in the file that the Executive Action Capability or ZRRIFLE/QJWIN was ever used.)

April 1962

Edwards recalls Harvey contacting him in April and asking to be put in touch with Roselli. Edwards says that he verified Helms' approval and then made the arrangements. Harvey states that he briefed Helms before his first meeting with Roselli, explaining its purpose, and that he also reported to Helms the results of his meeting with Roselli. Harvey states that thereafter he regularly briefed Helms on the status of the Castro operation.

(Comment: Edwards' statement that he "verified Helms' approval" is the earliest indication we have that Mr. Helms had been made witting of the gambling syndicate operation against Castro. Harvey added that, when he briefed Helms on Roselli, he obtained Helms' approval not to brief the Director.)

Edwards, Harvey, and O'Connell have differing recollections of the specifics of the turnover from Edwards/O'Connell to Harvey. Not all of the differences can be resolved — not even by follow-up interviews in which the information furnished by each was checked with each of the other two. There is no disagreement on the fact of the turnover nor on when it took place. The recollections vary decidedly, though, on the status of the operation at the time of its transfer to Harvey and on just how clean the break was between phase one under Edwards and phase two under Harvey.

a. Edwards believes that the operation was called off completely after the Bay of Pigs and that there was no further operational activity in connection with it until Harvey met Roselli and reactivated the operation in April 1962. O'Connell introduced Harvey to Roselli, and Edwards had nothing further to do with the operation — with the exception of a meeting with Attorney General Robert Kennedy in connection with the Phyllis

McGuire wiretapping incident. (The wiretapping incident is described in a separate section of this report.) Edwards' records show that on 14 May 1962 Harvey called Edwards "and indicated that he was dropping any plans for the use of Roselli for the future."

b. Harvey's recollection of the turnover tends to support Edwards' summary, but he claims that he took over "a going operation." Some support for this claim is found in his description of just how it was planned to get the poison into Castro's food by employing someone with access to a restaurant frequented by Castro. The mechanics were identical with those described by Edwards and as reported in our earlier account of phase one of the operation.

c. O'Connell's account of his own role in the operation in the early weeks following Harvey's supposed takeover makes it evident that there was not a clean break between the Office of Security's responsibility and that of Harvey. Further, O'Connell now believes that there must have been "something going on" between April 1961 (after the Bay of Pigs) and April 1962, but he claims to be unable to remember any of the particulars.

There are other disagreements among the three on facts. They are reviewed here, not because they alter the essential fact of the turnover or of Harvey's sole responsibliity for the operation after a certain point in time, but because they suggest that persons who were supposedly unwitting of events after the turnover were in fact witting, because they were not effectively cut off at the instant of turnover.

Harvey's notes show that he and O'Connell went to New York City to meet Roselli on the 8th and 9th of April 1962. O'Connell recalls it as being early in April and that the introduction was made on a Sunday, which would make it the 8th. Harvey says that only he and O'Connell met with Roselli; O'Connell says that Maheu was also present at the meeting. Both are positive of the accuracy of their recollections, and each gives reasons for his confidence in his clarity of recall. The significance, for purposes of this inquiry, is whether Maheu did or did not know that the operation continued under Harvey.

a. Harvey is certain that he would have remembered it if Maheu were present. He and Maheu were in the same FBI training class at Quantico in 1940. He does not remember having seen Maheu since he, Harvey, came with the Agency in 1947, although he acknowledges that he may have seen him once or twice socially. He is sure he has not seen Maheu since 1952 when Harvey was assigned to Berlin.

b. O'Connell, who set up the meeting, is just as positive that Maheu was there. He describes a series of events that reassure him of the accuracy of his memory. The four of them traveled separately to New York. They met at the Savoy Plaza Hotel (Savoy Hilton?) where all four stayed. After discussions, Maheu suggested dinner at the Elk Room, a fashionable restaurant in a nearby hotel. O'Connell says that Maheu picked up the tab. They finished dinner about 9:30 or 10:00 p.m. Roselli wanted to buy the group a nightcap, but since it was Sunday night nearly all of the bars were closed. They walked around the neighborhood looking for an open bar and finally wound up at the Copacabana. They were refused admittance to the bar because of a rule restricting admission to couples, so they sat at a table where they could watch the floor show. Roselli found himself facing a table at "ringside" at which Phyllis McGuire was sitting with Dorothy Kilgallen and Liberace for the opening night of singer Rosemary Clooney. To avoid Phyllis McGuire's seeing him, Roselli got his companions to change their seating arrangement so that his back was turned to Miss McGuire. Maheu was an integral part of all this. (Roselli's reason for not wanting Phyllis McGuire to see him with his companions will become evident from her role in the wiretapping incident, which is described in a separate section of this report.)

The two differing recollections cannot be reconciled. As a point of interest, Edwards stated that when he briefed Harvey on the operation he deliberately omitted reference to Maheu in order to screen Maheu off from Harvey's takeover of the operation.

The next significant point of difference has to do with what happened after the New York meeting. O'Connell told us that he and Roselli left New York for Miami the next day (presumably 10 April) and remained there until Harvey arrived. Harvey, on the other hand, recalls a meeting with O'Connell and Roselli in Washington on 14 April. O'Connell, at first, did not recall the Washington meeting, but, when given Harvey's chronology, he said he did recall returning to Washington to meet Harvey for some purpose but that the details are vague in his mind. Harvey at first thought that the 14 April meeting in Washington was O'Connell's last contact with Roselli during this second phase of the gambling syndicate operation. O'Connell told us that Roselli was apprehensive over the new arrangement (and of Harvey personally) and asked O'Connell to remain on for a time, which O'Connell agreed to do. When told that O'Connell was sure that he had continued on in the operation for some two or three weeks after Harvey's takeover, Harvey agreed that this was correct. O'Connell's carryover was for purposes of continuity. We cannot be sure of the date O'Connell was finally eliminated from the operation. He was in Miami with Roselli and Harvey perhaps as late as 27 April. His role in the operation had definitely ended by June 1962 when he was assigned PCS to Okinawa.

Harvey recalls leaving Washington for Miami by automobile on 19 April. He thought that he took delivery of the pills from Dr. Gunn before leaving. Gunn has no record of any such delivery at that time; his last record concerning pills is dated February 1961. ██████████ does have a notation of delivering four pills (one capsule and three tablets) to "J. O." on 18 April 1962. ██████████ reads this as being Jim O'Connell. When told of this, Harvey agreed that it was probably correct. O'Connell also feels that he must have been in Washington for the pill delivery.

Harvey says that he arrived in Miami on 21 April 1962 and found Roselli already in touch with Tony Varona, the Cuban exile leader who had participated in phase one. It is at this point that the final difference in recollections occurs. Harvey described the manner in which the lethal material was to be introduced into Castro's food, involving an asset of Varona's who had access to someone in a restaurant frequented by Castro. We told Harvey that Edwards had described precisely the same plan. When we asked Harvey how Edwards could have known of the mechanics if there had been no activity in the operation for a year, and if Harvey was starting again from scratch, Harvey replied that he took over a going operation — one that was already "in train." Edwards denies that this is so. O'Connell says that Harvey is the one who is right. The operation was going on when Harvey took it over, although O'Connell does not remember when Varona was reactivated or what had been done with him in the meantime.

Along with the change in Agency leadership of the operation, which saw Harvey replacing Edwards/O'Connell, there also were changes in the original cast of hoodlum players. Harvey specified that Giancana was not to be brought in on the reactivation of the operation, and he believes that Roselli honored the request. Roselli once reported to Harvey that Giancana had asked if anything was going on, and when Roselli said that nothing was happening, Giancana said, "Too bad." Additionally, Santos Trafficante ("Joe, the courier" from the earlier phase) was no longer involved. With the closing of the last casino in Havana in September 1961, Trafficante presumably no longer had access. Roselli now had a man known to Harvey as Maceo, who also used the names Garcia-Gomez and Godoy.

(Comment: Harvey is unable further to identify Maceo; he describes him as "a Cuban who spoke Italian." One of Varona's associates in the Cuban exile community was named Antonio MACEO Mackle, but it seems unlikely that he was the Maceo of this operation. He was prominent enough in the exile community to have been known to Harvey. Further, it seems clear that Maceo was "Roselli's man." This second phase appears to lack the overwhelming, high-level gangster flavor that characterized the first phase. Roselli remained as a prominent figure in the operation, but working directly with the Cuban exile community and directly on behalf of CIA. Roselli was essential to the second phase as a contact with Varona, who presumably still believed he was being supported by U.S. businessmen with financial stakes in Cuba. Roselli needed Giancana and Trafficante in the first phase as a means of establishing contacts inside Cuba. He did not need them in the second phase, because he had Varona. However, it would be naive to assume that Roselli did not take the precaution of informing higher-ups in the syndicate that he was working in a territory considered to be the private domain of someone else in the syndicate.)

When the pills were given to Varona through Roselli, Varona requested arms and equipment needed for the support of his end of the operation. Roselli passed the request to Harvey. Harvey, with the help of Ted Shackley, the chief of the JMWAVE Station, procured explosives, detonators, twenty .30 caliber rifles, twenty .45 caliber hand guns, two radios, and one boat radar. Harvey says that the "shopping list" included some items that could be obtained only from the U.S. Government. Harvey omitted those items, because Roselli, posing as a representative of private business interests, would not have had access to such equipment. The cost of the arms and equipment, about $5,000, was T/A'd to headquarters.

Harvey and Shackley rented a U-Haul truck under an assumed name, loaded it with the arms and equipment, and parked it in the parking lot of a drive-in restaurant. The keys were then given to Roselli for delivery either to Maceo, to Varona, or to Varona's son-in-law. Evidently Harvey and Roselli had not yet come to trust each other. Perhaps fearing a double-cross, each set about independently to assure himself that the equipment reached the proper hands. After parking the truck, Harvey and Shackley kept the parking lot under surveillance until the pass was completed. Roselli, accompanied by O'Connell, did the same. Neither pair knew that the other was watching. Eventually the truck was picked up and driven away. It was returned later, empty, and with the keys under the seat as prearranged. Harvey returned it to the rental agency. Harvey says that Shackley never knew to whom delivery was made nor for what purpose. Shackley was merely called upon to furnish support for a headquarters operation from which he was otherwise excluded.

May 1962

Harvey and Roselli arranged a system of telephone communication by which Harvey was kept posted on any developments. Harvey, using a pay phone, could call Roselli at the Friars Club in Los Angeles at 1600 hours, Los Angeles time. Roselli could phone Harvey at Harvey's home in the evening. Roselli reported that the pills were in Cuba and at the restaurant reportedly used regularly by Castro.

June 1962

Roselli reported to Harvey on 21 June that Varona had dispatched a team of three men to Cuba. Just what they were supposed to do is pretty vague. Harvey said that they appeared to have no specific plan for killing Castro. They were to recruit others who might be used in such a scheme. If an opportunity to kill Castro presented itself, they or the persons they recruited were to make the attempt — perhaps using the pills. Harvey never learned their names or anything else about them. From the sequence of the reports, it would seem that the pills were sent in ahead of the three-man team, but this is not now ascertainable.

September 1962

Harvey saw Roselli in Miami on 7 and on 11 September. Varona was reported as then ready to send in another team of three men. They were supposedly militia men whose assignment was to penetrate Castro's body guard. During this period the "medicine" was reported as still in place and the three men of the first team safe.

September 1962-January 1963

Although Harvey received several reports that the militia men were poised to take off, presumably from somewhere in the Florida keys, they did not actually leave. First, "conditions inside" were given as the reason for delay; then the October missile crisis threw plans awry. Harvey was in Miami between 22 December and 6 January. He saw both Roselli and Maceo several times during that period. He made a payment of $2,700 to Roselli for passing to Varona for the expenses of the three militia men. Harvey and Roselli had telephone discussions of the operation between 11 and 16 January. Harvey says that Roselli wasn't kidding himself. He agreed with Harvey that nothing was happening and that there was not much chance that anything would happen in the future. As far as Harvey knows, the three militia men never did leave for Cuba. He knows nothing of what may have happened to the three reported to have been sent to Cuba.

February 1963

Harvey was in Miami 11-14 February. He had no contacts with any of the principals, but he left word for Maceo that there was nothing new and that it now looked as if it were all over. (Just how Harvey left this word for Maceo is not clear.)

Harvey left Miami on 15 February to meet with Roselli in Los Angeles. They agreed at the Los Angeles meeting that the operation would be closed off, but that it would be unwise to attempt a precipitate break between Roselli and Varona. Roselli agreed that he would continue to see Varona, gradually reducing the frequency of contact until there was none.

April-May 1963

Harvey says that he received two telephone calls from Roselli during this period. Harvey decided that it would be best to have one last meeting with Roselli before he left for his assignment in ■■■■■. He states that he reported this decision to Mr. Helms who gave his approval.

June 1963

Roselli came to Washington to meet with Harvey sometime about the middle of June. Harvey met him at Dulles airport. Harvey remembers having suggested to Roselli that he bring only carry-on luggage so there would be no delay at the airport awaiting baggage. Harvey had by then closed his own home in preparation for leaving the country and was living in the house of a neighbor who was out of town. Roselli stayed with Harvey as a houseguest in the neighbor's home. That evening Roselli, Harvey, and Mrs. Harvey went out for dinner. While dining, Harvey received a phone call from Sam Papich who wanted to know if Harvey knew the identity of his dinner guest. Harvey said that he did.

It subsequently developed that the FBI had Roselli under intensive surveillance at the time, and Harvey speculates that he was picked up as he left the airport parking lot and was identified through his auto license number. Harvey met Papich for breakfast the next morning and explained that he was terminating an operational association with Roselli. Papich reminded Harvey of the FBI rule requiring FBI personnel to report any known contacts between former FBI employees and criminal elements. Papich said that he would have to report to J. Edgar Hoover that Harvey had been seen with Roselli. Harvey said he understood Papich's situation and did not object to such a report being made. Harvey said that he asked Papich to inform him in advance if it appeared that Hoover might call Mr. McCone — Harvey's point being that he felt that McCone should be briefed before receiving a call from Hoover. Papich agreed to do so. Harvey said that he then told Mr. Helms of the incident and that Helms agreed that there was no need to brief McCone unless a call from Hoover was to be expected.

This was Harvey's last face-to-face meeting with Roselli, although he has heard from him since then. The later links between Harvey and Roselli are described in a separate section of this report.

The list of persons witting of the second phase of the operation differs from those who knew of the first phase. Those we have identified are:

1. Richard Helms, Deputy Director for Plans

2. William Harvey, Chief, Task Force W

3. James O'Connell, Office of Security (He knows that Harvey took over the operation and delivered pills, arms, and equipment in April 1962. He does not know of developments after May 1962.)

4. Sheffield Edwards, Director of Security (He knows of the fact of the turnover to Harvey, but states he knows nothing of developments thereafter.)

5. J.C. King, Chief, WH Division (He stated in our interview with him that he knew that Harvey was having meetings with members of the gambling syndicate in 1962.)

6. ▆▆▆▆▆ Harvey's deputy in 1962 (▆▆▆ knows that Harvey was meeting with gangsters in Reno (sic) in the winter of 1962.)

7. Ted Shackley, Chief, JMWAVE (He assisted Harvey in the delivery of arms and equipment to Varona in April 1962, but

presumably did not know the identities of the recipients nor the purpose for which the material was to be used.)

8. ███████ TSD ██████s participation was limited to furnishing the pills to O'Connell on 18 April 1962.)

9. Antonio Varona, the Cuban exile leader (He presumably was not aware of government sponsorship.)

10. Varona's son-in-law (He too was presumably not aware of the government's role.)

11. Maceo, Roselli's "man" (Maceo probably knew there was a government connection, but may not have identified CIA as the agency.)

We can only conjecture as to who else may have known at least that the operation was continuing and perhaps some of the details. Sam Giancana was supposedly cut out of the second phase, but we cannot be sure that Roselli did not keep him informed. The same may be said of Santos Trafficante. Harvey is sure that Maheu was not involved in Harvey's introduction to Roselli, but O'Connell is equally positive that Maheu participated. The story that Drew Pearson told the President, and which is known in other Government circles, sounds suspiciously like this second phase of the operation. If that is so, then it is likely that the operation has leaked — perhaps through these channels:

Roselli to Maheu
Maheu to Edward P. Morgan, Maheu's Washington lawyer
Morgan to Drew Pearson
Pearson to Chief Justice Warren and to the President
Warren to Rowley, chief of the Secret Service
Rowley to Pat Coyne and to the FBI
The FBI to Attorney General Clark

We have a more detailed treatment in a separate section of this report of the channels through which the story may have passed.

The Wiretapping Incident

Late 1961-Early 1962

Well after the Pre-Bay of Pigs phase of the gambling syndicate operation to assassinate Castro, and only indirectly related to it, a development in the private life of Sam Giancana led to an incident that made the FBI aware of the Agency's relationship with the syndicate and required the briefing of the Attorney General on the details of the assassination plan.

Phyllis McGuire, of the singing McGuire sisters, was and is openly known to be Giancana's mistress. Giancana suspected her of having an affair with Dan Rowan, of the Rowan and Martin comedy team. Both Rowan and Miss McGuire were then entertaining in Las Vegas, and Giancana asked Maheu to put a bug in Rowan's room. Maheu did not want to do the job and declined on the grounds that he wasn't equipped for that sort of work. Giancana made a claim for a return favor: he had worked on the Castro assassination operation for Maheu, and Maheu was indebted to him. Giancana said that if Maheu wouldn't take on the job, he, Giancana, would go to Las Vegas and do it himself. Maheu agreed to arrange to have the room bugged.

(Comment: The exact date of this is uncertain. An August 1963 item on Giancana in the Chicago Sun-Times refers to the incident, without mention of wiretapping, and sets the year as 1961. There is nothing in Agency files that pinpoints the date, and the memories of those we interviewed who know of the incident are hazy. Edwards and O'Connell did not learn of the incident until after it had happened. Edwards can place it only as being after the Bay of Pigs. O'Connell at first thought that it was in early 1962. When shown the newspaper account, O'Connell said that if the news story was correct, it would have had to have been very late in 1961. An Office of Security memorandum to the DDCI, of June 1966, states that it was "at the height of the project negotiations." This is confusing, rather than clarifying, because the operation was supposedly at dead standstill in late 1961 and very early 1962. Clearly the incident occurred before 7 February 1962, because it was on that date that the Director of Security told the FBI that CIA would object to prosecution. Presumably the FBI's case was already complete by then.)

Maheu arranged to have Giancana's request handled by Edward L. Du Bois, a private investigator in Miami. Du Bois assigned two men to the job: Arthur J. Balletti and J.W. Harrison.

(Comment: The September 1966 classified telephone directory for the Greater Miami Area lists Edward L. Du Bois under "Detective Agencies." There is an advertisment on the page for "Arthur J. Balletti Investigations" which lists as one of his specialities the obtaining of photographic and electronic evidence.)

O'Connell recalls that, instead of planting a microphone in Rowan's room, the investigator tapped the telephone, which would not have revealed the sort of intimacies that Giancana expected to discover. When Rowan left the room to do a show, Balletti also left his room to see the act, leaving his equipment out in full sight and running. It was found by a maid, and the local sheriff's office was called. Balletti was arrested. Harrison was not picked up. Agency personnel have no further information about Harrison. The FBI identified him only as being "supplied by Maheu".

Balletti first tried to telephone Du Bois for help but could not reach him. He then called Maheu, in the presence of the sheriff's officers. O'Connell says that Maheu was able to fix the matter with local Las Vegas authorities, perhaps with help from Roselli. However, Balletti's call to Maheu caused the case to reach the FBI. The Bureau decided to press for prosecution under the wiretapping statute. When Maheu was approached by the FBI, he referred them to the CIA Director of Security, Sheffield Edwards.

(Comment: Edwards states that he had told Maheu, who had to work closely with the thugs, that if he got into a bind with the FBI, he could tell the Bureau that he was working on an intelligence operation being handled by Edwards. Maheu, according to Edwards, told the Bureau that he had not personally done the wiretapping, but that it grew out of an operation he was working on with Edwards. Maheu presumably did not mention the ultimate objective of the "intelligence operation" involving the gambling syndicate. The Bureau, in a memorandum from J. Edgar Hoover to the DCI, dated 23 March 1962, stated that: "Maheu claimed that he ordered coverage of Rowan in behalf of CIA's efforts to obtain intelligence information in Cuba through the hoodlum element, including Sam Giancana, which had interests there. Maheu said he was put in contact with Giancana in connection with these intelligence activities through John Roselli, a Los Angeles hoodlum. Maheu authorized wiring of Rowan's room and discussed this matter with John Roselli.")

March 1962

The 23 March memorandum from the Bureau takes the form of a letter of confirmation of a 7 February meeting between an unnamed representative of the FBI and Shef Edwards. The memorandum quotes Edwards as having made the following points: Maheu was involved in a sensitive operation with the Agency; the Agency would object to any prosecution that would necessitate use of CIA personnel or information; and introduction of evidence concerning CIA operations would embarrass the Government. This is also essentially as stated to us by Edwards in reviewing the incident during the course of this investigation.

The 23 March memorandum stated that the Criminal Division of the Department of Justice requested that CIA advise specifically if it objected to initiation of criminal prosecution against Balletti, Maheu, and Harrison. On 28 or 29 March, Edwards met with the Bureau liason officer, Sam Papich, and told him that any prosecution would endanger sensitive sources and methods used in a duly authorized project and would not be in the national interest. Papich accepted Edwards' oral statement as the reply requested and said that he would report to proper authorities in the Bureau. Edwards made a record of the meeting in a memorandum of 4 April 1962.

Edwards informed us during our inquiry that at the time of the bugging incident and the flap that ensued those (Dulles and Bissell) who had given the initial approval of the plan to assassinate Castro through the gambling syndicate were gone. As no one else in authority (including Mr. Helms) had been cut in on the operation, Edwards dealt with Papich without reference to anyone else in the Agency.

April 1962

In early April Papich informed Edwards that Herbert J. Miller, Assistant Attorney General in charge of the Criminal Division of the Department of Justice, wanted to discuss the case. Edwards then brought in Lawrence Houston, General Counsel, and asked Houston to call on Miller and tell him that the bugging incident in Las Vegas was related to an intelligence operation and that the Agency did not think it wise at that time to surface its connection with Roselli.

Houston met with Miller on 16 April and told him of the Agency's invovement, without revealing any details of the assassination operation. Houston's memorandum of the meeting, dated 26 April, quotes Miller as saying that he foresaw no major difficulty in stopping prosecution, but that he might mention the problem to the Attorney General. Houston's memorandum notes that Miller raised a question about the possibility of our involvement in this particular case, the Las Vegas wiretap, standing in the way of prosecution of other actions, particularly against Giancana.

Houston's 26 April memorandum states that on 20 April there was a second meeting with Justice — with Miller's first assistant, Mr. Foley. At that meeting Houston told Foley that the Agency's request not to prosecute was limited to this specific bugging incident, was based on security grounds, and that security considerations would not be a bar to prosecution on other matters. As it was possible that the Attorney General might be told about this and might then call the DCI, Houston briefed the DDCI, General Carter, who said he understood the situation and in due time might brief the Director, Mr. McCone. It is not known whether General Carter did or did not brief Mr. McCone. There is no indication that General Carter was further briefed on the full details of the assassination plot against Castro.

May 1962

The Attorney General obviously was told of CIA's operational involvement with gangster elements, because he requested a briefing on the details. On 7 May 1962 Sheffield Edwards and Lawrence Houston met with Attorney General Robert Kennedy and, as Edwards puts it, "briefed him all the way." Houston says that after the briefing Kennedy "thought about the problem quite seriously." The Attorney General said that he could see the problem and that he could not proceed against those involved in the wiretapping case. He spoke quite firmly, saying in effect, "I trust that if you ever try to do business with organized crime again — with gangsters — you will let the Attorney General know before you do it." Houston quotes Edwards as replying that this was a reasonable request. Edwards says that among the points covered was that of Roselli's motivation. The Attorney General had thought that Roselli was doing the job (the attempt at assassination of Castro) for money. Edwards corrected that impression; he was not.

Houston recalls that during the meeting with the Attorney General the latter asked for a memorandum record of the meeting. Edwards believes that the request was made later and by telephone. A memorandum was prepared and was signed by Edwards. Both Edwards and Houston recall having had a hand in writing it. A transmittal buck-slip from Houston to Kennedy notes that the request was made on 11 May, which suggests that Edwards is correct in his belief that the request was made by telephone after the 7 May briefing of the Attorney General. The memorandum is dated 14 May 1962. It was typed in two copies only, with the original being sent to Attorney General Kennedy and the other copy being retained by the Director of Security. It was typed by Edwards' secretary, Sarah Hall. It does not state the purpose of the operation on which Kennedy was briefed, but it does make it clear that the operation was against Castro and its true purpose may be inferrred from the memorandum.

Edwards states that the briefing of the Attorney General and the forwarding of a memorandum of record was carried out without briefing the Director (John McCone), the DDCI (General Carter), or the DD/P (Richard Helms). He felt that, since they had not been privy to the operation when it was under way, they should be protected from involvement in it after the fact. As noted previously, Houston had briefed the DDCI on the fact that there was a matter involving the Department of Justice, but Houston had not given the DDCI the specifics. He feels it would have been normal for him to have briefed the DCI in view of the Attorney General's interest, but he also feels quite sure that he would have remembered doing it and he does not. He suggested that Edwards' deliberate avoidance of such briefings may have led him also to avoid making any briefings. He recalls no disagreements with Edwards on this point and concludes that he must have accepted Edwards' decision not to brief.

Houston and Edwards briefed Robert Kennedy on a CIA operation embracing gangster elements, which presumably was terminated following the Bay of Pigs fiasco. Kennedy stated his view, reportedly quite strongly, that the Attorney General should be told in advance of any future CIA intentions to work with or through U.S. gangster elements. From reports of the briefing, it is reasonable to assume that Kennedy believed he had such a commitment from Agency representatives.

In fact, however, at the time of the 7 May 1962 briefing of the Attorney General on "Gambling Syndicate — Phase One," Phase Two under William Harvey was already well under way. Harvey had been introduced to Roselli on 8 April and Varona or his men had received the lethal pills, the arms, and related support equipment in late April. The Attorney General was not told that the gambling syndicate operation had already been reactivated, nor, as far as we know, was he ever told that CIA had a continuing involvement with U.S. gangster elements.

When the Attorney General was briefed on 7 May, Edwards knew that Harvey had been introduced to Roselli. He must also have known that his subordinate, James O'Connell, was in Miami and roughly for what purpose (although Edwards does not now recall this). The gambling syndicate operation had been taken from him, and, in retrospect, he probably acted properly in briefing the Attorney General on only that aspect of the operation for which he had been responsible and of which he had direct, personal knowledge.

Harvey states that on 14 May he briefed Mr. Helms on the meeting with the Attorney General, as told to him by Edwards. Harvey, too, advised against briefing Mr. McCone and General Carter and states that Helms concurred in this. On that same date, 14 May, Edwards prepared a memorandum for the record stating that on that day Harvey had told him that any plans for future use of Roselli were dropped. Edwards' memorandum states that he "cautioned him (Harvey) that I (Edwards) felt that any future projects of this nature should have the tacit approval of the Director of Central Intelligence." Edwards informed us that he has no specific recollection of having told Harvey of Kennedy's warning that the Attorney General should be told in advance of any future CIA use of gangsters.

Although the Attorney General on 7 May 1962 was given a full and frank account of the Agency's relations with Maheu, Roselli, and Giancana in the Castro operation, including the wiretapping flap, it appears that the FBI was not given anything like the same detail. The Bureau quite properly was not told about the assassination operation, and it seems that it also was not told how the private life of Giancana came to involve the Agency in the Las Vegas wiretapping incident. Edwards states that to have briefed the Bureau on the assassination operation would have put it in an impossible bind, since both Roselli and Giancana were high on the Bureau's "list."

The briefing of Attorney General Kennedy was absolutely restricted to him, and we can only speculate that the confidence was observed.

(Comment: Senator Robert Kennedy's secretary, who was also his secretary when he was Attorney General, phoned the Director's office on 4 March 1967 and asked for a copy of the Edwards' memorandum on the 7 May 1962 meeting with Kennedy when he was Attorney General, at which time he was briefed on the Castro assassination operation. Kennedy knew of the Drew Pearson article of 7 March 1967 and wanted to check his recollection of what he had been told by Edwards and Houston on 7 May 1962. The Attorney General's copy of the memorandum for the record of that briefing is in the archives of the Attorney General's office. Mr. Helms subsequently had lunch with Senator Kennedy. He took a copy of the memorandum with him and allowed Kennedy to read it. He did not leave a copy with Kennedy.)

If the information given the Bureau is as limited as the records and our information indicate, then the Bureau has not been informed, as the Attorney General was, that the Agency was first unwitting and then a reluctant accessory after the fact. It would be surprising, though, if the Bureau does not now know the whole story of the Las Vegas bugging incident. Whether the Bureau may now think that CIA was less than candid about the bugging incident (as distinguished from the sensitive assassination operation) is a question for speculation.

August 1963

What is available to the press is undoubtedly available to the Bureau. In fact, some indication of the extent of the Bureau's knowledge is found in a feature story in the *Chicago Sun-Times* of 16 August 1963, with a Washington date line, under the banner lead:

"CIA SOUGHT GIANCANA HELP FOR CUBA SPYING"

The article cites "Justice Department sources" as expressing the belief that Giancana never did any spying at all for the CIA. He merely pretended to go along with the CIA:

"in the hope that the Justice Department's drive to put him behind bars might be slowed — or at least affected — by his ruse of co-operation with another government agency."

The story places the period of the relationship from 1959 to:

"some time in 1960, long before the abortive rebel invasion at the Bay of Pigs in April, 1961."

The newspaper then gives the following version of the bugging incident:

"An equally bizarre episode months later gave the Justice Department its first clue to Giancana's negotiation with the CIA.

"The figures in this incident were a male night-club entertainer and Giancana's girl friend, Phyllis McGuire, one of the singing McGuire sisters.

"At the time, in Giancana's opinion, the entertainer was overly attentive to Miss McGuire.

"At Las Vegas, Nev., in 1961, sheriff's police seized a prowler in the entertainer's hotel suite. For hours, the intruder refused to identify himself or say he was rifling the entertainer's rooms.

"Persistent questioning by sheriff's deputies, according to federal authorities, led to an admission by the prowler that he was on the payroll of a private detective agency in Florida.

"Florida authorities sought an explanation of the incident from the operator of the detective agency. At first, the operator refused to discuss the matter. Finally, however, he told investigators to get in touch with the CIA.

"The inquiry then shifted from Florida to Washington and revealed Giancana's negotiations with CIA, it was disclosed.

"Government sources reported Thursday that the private investigator's mission in the Las Vegas suite of the entertainer was another riddle of the Giancana caper with the CIA. Neither CIA nor the Florida detective agency ever has offered an explanation of what the investigator was doing in the hotel suite, the sources said."

Four days later, on 20 August 1963, the *Chicago Daily News* reported further on the subject under the following headline:

"THE TRUTH ABOUT COSA NOSTRA CHIEF AND THE CIA"

The story cited an incident in which Giancana literally bumped into an FBI agent who was tailing him. Giancana was reported to have said, "Why don't you fellows leave me alone? I'm one of you!" Giancana is represented in the newspaper account as having been approached by — but not as having made any arrangements with — CIA. The story also mentions the Las Vegas incident, but in terms of someone, possibly CIA, ransacking a room occupied by one of Giancana's henchmen who had just returned from Cuba.

On 16 August 1963 the DD/P (Helms) sent a memorandum to the DCI (McCone) forwarding a copy of the 14 May 1962 memorandum for the record sent to Attorney General Kennedy following the 7 May 1962 briefing of Kennedy on the gambling syndicate operation — phase one. The coincidence of dates strongly suggests that the Director's interest resulted from the Chicago newspaper story of 16 August. In his transmittal memorandum to the DCI, Mr. Helms wrote that:

"... I was vaguely aware of the existence of such a memorandum (the memorandum for the record of the 7 May 1962 briefing of Robert Kennedy) since I was informed that it had been written as a result of a briefing given by Colonel Edwards and Lawrence Houston to the Attorney General in May of last year ... I assume you are aware of the nature of the operation discussed in the attachment."

This is the earliest date on which we have evidence of Mr. McCone's being aware of any aspect of the scheme to assassinate Castro using members of the gambling syndicate.

Drew Pearson has access to these newspaper stories, and they are available to any number of sources who might wish to collect such information. The rumors of CIA's alliance with gangsters are not new; what is new is that the rumors now connect CIA and the gangsters in a plot to assassinate Castro. It may be assumed that the Attorney General (Clark) knows that the rumors of the relationship, as such, are true because of the records of the FBI on the Las Vegas wiretapping incident. As of this writing, he does not necessarily know more — subject to what he may have learned as a result of the FBI interview of Edward P. Morgan, Maheu's Washington attorney. A clue as to how much the Attorney General may know is found in his statement that Maheu is the closest thing to a link between CIA and Giancana.

May-July 1966

The Long Committee

The Agency's previous interventions on Maheu's behalf are reviewed here, because of the increasingly important role of Maheu in the scenario. The last of these interventions occurred during the period May-June 1966. At that time a Senate Committee headed by Senator Long of Missouri was investigating invasions of privacy and planned to call Maheu to testify. We learned indirectly of the Committee's intention to call him. A man who was employed by Maheu in 1954-55 was informed that he would be called to testify about his activities during that period. He was an employee of AID in 1966. The Internal Security Division of the Department of Justice learned that he was to be called as a witness and informed CIA's General Counsel.

In the 1954-55 time period Maheu was hired by the Greek shipping magnate, Niarchos, to help in a financial tussle Niarchos was having with another Greek shipping figure, Onassis, who had managed to negotiate a pact with King Saud under which Onassis would control 90% of all Saudi Arabian oil shipments. British, American, and German shipping interests opposed Onassis' near monopoly, and the US and UK governments supported Niarchos in his fight to have the agreement cancelled. Maheu is believed to have worked at top levels in both the British and American governments, reportedly meeting at least once with Vice President Nixon. Maheu's operations were financed by Niarchos, but CIA became involved in supporting them by request of the Department of State. Agency communications and pouch facilities were made available to Maheu, and he was given help in developing a black propaganda campaign against Onassis. Niarchos, with Maheu's help, won his scrap with Onassis.

A variety of litigation arose from the contest. In one law suit for libel before the New York Supreme Court in early 1956 (Onassis vs. Catapodis), Niarchos was examined by attorneys for Catapodis.

When questions were asked about certain affidavits in issue (which had been passed through the CIA pouch system), Niarchos, as a witness, was advised by his attorneys not to testify on the grounds of Government privilege. CIA inevitably became involved. The General Counsel prepared a statement for the U.S. District Attorney in New York (to be retained by the OO/C office there) stating the Agency's interest. As a consequence, CIA was identified as being a party to the Niarchos/Onassis squabble. Although that was in 1956, the Agency's intervention is presumably still a matter of record.

The Long Committee planned to resurrect the old Onassis/Niarchos fight, because it had involved an invasion of privacy. Apparently one of the things Maheu did was to hire someone to run a technical surveillance on Onassis' offices, and this became known. Maheu's more recent involvement in the Las Vegas wiretapping incident also seemed certain to receive extensive attention by the Long Committee.

The Long Committee presumably would have been interested only in Maheu's connection with the wiretappings that grew out of the Onassis/Niarchos affair and the gambling syndicate operation against Castro. The Agency decided that it would not be in its interest to allow Maheu to testify on the bugging incidents because of the risk that his testimony could not be confined just to wiretapping. Further, Maheu has been used over the years in a number of sensitive CIA operations. There was a risk that a general inquiry might open up other sensitive issues. A number of meetings were held with Edward P. Morgan, Maheu's Washington attorney, and with a close legal associate of Senator Long, a St. Louis attorney named Morris Shenker. Finally, in direct meetings with Senator Long, our General Counsel was able to have Maheu excused from testifying before the Long Committee.

While negotiations were under way to have Maheu excused from testifying, Maheu became quite alarmed over the risk of adverse publicity, which might jeopardise his business with very important clients. He was especially worried over his Howard Hughes account. He applied pressure on the Agency in a variety of ways — suggesting that publicity might expose his past sensitive work for CIA. Maheu's background and past associations with CIA are the subject of another section of this report.

James O'Connell states that at one point in the negotiations with the Long Committee <u>Maheu indicated that he might brief his attorney, Edward P. Morgan, fully about his past activities so that Morgan would be able to decide how best to represent him.</u> Whether he did or not, and, if so, what he told him, is not known. We have a discussion of the possible implications of this in a later section of this report.

a. Maheu may very well have told Morgan the details of the plan to assassinate Castro using members of the gambling syndicate, and

b. Maheu has now, on three separate occasions, seen CIA intervene in official proceedings — once for Niarchos and twice for Maheu.

Schemes in Early 1963

Skin Diving Suits

At about the time of the Donovan-Castro negotiations for the release of the Bay of Pigs prisoners a plan was devised to have Donovan present a contaminated skin diving suit to Castro as a gift. Castro was known to be a skin diving enthusiast. We cannot put a precise date on this scheme. Desmond FitzGerald told us of it as if it had originated after he took over the Cuba task force in January 1963. Samuel Halpern said that it began under William Harvey and that he, Halpern, briefed FitzGerald on it. Harvey states positively that he never heard of it.

According to Sidney Gottlieb, this scheme progressed to the point of actually buying a diving suit and readying it for delivery. The technique involved dusting the inside of the suit with a fungus that would produce a disabling and chronic skin disease (Madura foot) and contaminating the breathing apparatus with tubercle bacilli. Gottlieb does not remember what came of the scheme or what happened to the scuba suit. Sam Halpern, who was in on the scheme, at first said the plan was dropped because it was obviously impracticable. He later recalled that the plan was abandoned because it was overtaken by events: Donovan had already given Castro a skin diving suit on his own initiative. The scheme may have been mentioned to Mike Miskovsky, who worked with Donovan, but FitzGerald has no recollection that it was.

Halpern says that he mentioned the plan to George McManus, then a special assistant to the DD/P (Helms). McManus later told Halpern that he had mentioned the scheme to Mr. Helms. Those who were involved in the plot or who were indentified to us by the participants as being witting are the following:

>   Richard Helms
>   William Harvey (denies any knowledge)
>   Desmond FitzGerald
>   Samuel Halpern
>   George McManus
>   Sidney Gottlieb
>   ███████████.

Booby-trapped Sea Shell

Some time in 1963, date uncertain but probably early in the year, Desmond FitzGerald, then Chief, SAS, originated a scheme for doing away with Castro by means of an explosives-rigged sea shell. The idea was to take an unusually spectacular sea shell that would be certain to catch Castro's eye, load it with an explosive triggered to blow when the shell was lifted, and submerge it in an area where Castro often went skin diving.

Des bought two books on Caribbean Mollusca. The scheme was soon found to be impracticable. None of the shells that might conceivably be found in the Caribbean area was both spectacular enough to be sure of attracting attention and large enough to hold the needed volume of explosive. The midget submarine that would have had to be used in emplacement of the shell has too short an operating range for such an operation.

FitzGerald states that he, Sam Halpern, and ███████████ had several sessions at which they explored this possibility, but that no one else was ever brought in on the talks. Halpern believes that he had conversations with TSD on feasibility and using a hypothetical case. He does not remember with whom he may have spoken. We are unable to identify any others who knew of the scheme at the time it was being considered.

Project AMLASH — Rolando Cubela

9 March 1961

███████████, an officer then assigned to the Mexico City Station, met in Mexico City with Rolando Cubela to sound out Cubela on his views on the Cuban situation. Cubela had been attending the leftist-sponsored Latin American Conference on National Sovereignty, Emancipation and Peace held in Mexico City from 5 to 8 March. Cubela was noncommital. The meeting was arranged by ████████████ (AMWHIP-1), a long-time friend of Cubela. Cubela knew ██████ casually from Havana where ██████ was once assigned and where a similar meeting had once been set up but had fallen through.

(Comment: Rolando CUBELA Secades was the second-ranking leader of the Directorio Revolucionario (DR) 13 de Marzo, which was an elite group of leftist student activists founded in 1956 to organize violence to overthrow the Batista regime. Cubela was believed to have been one of the participants in the assassination in 1956 of Lt. Col. Antonio BLANCO Rico, then the head of Batista's military intelligence service. The DR members considered themselves quite apart from the Fidelista 26th of July Movement, despite the fact that they had reluctantly signed a unity pact. In the final days of the revolution the DR took the Presidential Palace, which they refused to surrender to Che Guevara but eventually (and reluctantly) turned over to Fidel Castro. Cubela was a major in the Cuban army, the highest Cuban military rank.

(A CS Information Report with a date of information of March 1959 reported that: "Prior to his appointment to the post of Cuban Military Attache to Spain and his subsequent departure for Madrid on 27 March 1959, Rolando Cubela frankly expressed to Prime Minister Fidel Castro his dissatisfaction over the present situation in Cuba. Cubela . . . privately told intimates that he was so disgusted with Castro that if he, Cubela, did not get out of the country soon, he would kill Castro himself."

(Although the March 1961 meeting between ▆▆▆▆ and Cubela in Mexico City was inconclusive, it led to other meetings out of which grew Project AMLASH. Cubela (AMLASH-1) repeatedly insisted that the essential first step in overthrowing the regime was the elimination of Castro himself, which Cubela claimed he was prepared to accomplish. He repeatedly requested that we furnish him the special equipment or material needed to do the job. Those immediately concerned with the running of the operation now recall it as one in which the Agency was interested primarily in keeping Cubela active in the ▆▆▆▆ program directed against Cuban military leaders, while resisting his pleas for technical assistance in an assassination attempt. The voluminous project files and the information furnished us by ▆▆▆▆▆▆, Cubela's case officer, do not wholly support those recollections. The Agency offered both direct and indirect support for Cubela's plottings.)

28 March 1961

An asset of the Miami Station reported that Rolando Cubela and Juan Orta wanted to defect and needed help in escaping. (Juan Orta was the gangsters' "man inside Cuba" with access to Castro in the lethal pill operation we have called Gambling Syndicate — Phase One.) Headquarters expressed interest in exfiltrating Orta and Cubela. The exfiltration attempt was called off as a result of a report that the Cuban police were aware of Cubela's desire to defect and of his departure plans.

(Comment: This is one of three name-links we found in the AMLASH file between Rolando Cubela and persons involved in the gambling syndicate episodes. The other two links are even more nebulous than this. If Cubela was in fact one of the gangsters' assets inside Cuba, that fact was unknown to either the CIA officers running the gangster episodes or to those handling Cubela.)

14 August 1961

██████████ reported that Rolando Cubela was planning to attend the French National Student Union Cultural Festival later in the month. Cubela sent a message to ██████ saying that he wanted to talk with a "friend of ████████████'s" in Paris if possible. The message presumably was passed through Cubela's girl friend, an airline stewardess. ████████ was given approval to approach Cubela, but there is no indication in the file that he was actually contacted.

15 June 1962

The JMWAVE Station cabled that a station asset ██████ was told by ████████████ that Cubela had left Cuba for Helsinki on 10 June 1962. He was traveling on a Czech airline, by way of Prague, to Helsinki where he planned to attend the World Youth Festival. ██████'s mother and father had arrived in Miami on 9 June and had been seen off at the airport by Cubela when they left Cuba. ██████'s mother told ██████ that Cubela wanted to defect and to enter the U.S. Cubela said that on his return from Helsinki he would pass through Paris where he hoped to meet his old friend, ████████████.

27 June 1962

The FBI forwarded to CIA a report of a meeting with an FBI informant in Miami on 11 June. The informant reported that Cubela was attending the Youth Festival in Helsinki in July-August 1962 and wanted to defect. In a detailed transmittal memorandum, the FBI identified its informant as ██████████ whom the FBI knew to be a long-time contact of CIA. ██████ offered his services to the FBI to assist in the defection of Cubela. He told the Bureau of ██████'s meeting with Cubela in Mexico City in March 1961. The Bureau stated in its memorandum to us that it had told ██████ that his offer would be forwarded to the proper U.S. agency. The Bureau also stated that it was informing its Paris representative to refer ██████ to CIA if ██████ should contact the Paris Legal Attache.

8 July 1962

The JMWAVE Station reported the substance of a telephone conversation between Tepedino and a station officer, which was arranged by ██████. Tepedino identified the original source of his information on Cubela's desire to defect as being the Echavarrias, from whom the JMWAVE Station had received its report. Tepedino said he had approached the FBI in Miami because of dissatisfaction with the way CIA had handled Cubela's "planned defection" in Paris in August 1961. ██████ agreed to meet with a CIA officer and contact arrangements were made.

13 and 14 July 1962

██████████████████ from headquarters, met with ██████ in New York City on 13 and 14 July 1962. ██████████ agreed to meet ██████████████ in Helsinki, and to travel anywhere else necessary, to aid in an attempt to defect Cubela. ██████, who is a successful Cuban exile ██████████ in New York City, refused an offer to pay his full expenses. He did accept reimbursement for airline tickets and hotel expenses. He was not offered a salary or bonus.

30 July-6 August 1962

██████ arrived in Helsinki on 30 July. ██████████ was already there. Cubela was found, and the first of a series of meetings with him was held on 1 August. The original objective of defecting Cubela was quickly changed to one of recruiting him in place. These are excerpts from ████'s contact report of the first meeting with Cubela:

> He said he was considering not going back to Cuba, but after talking to ██████ he felt that if he could do something really significant for the creation of a new Cuba, he was interested in returning to carry on the fight there.
>
> He said he was not interested in risking his life for any small undertaking, but that if he could be given a really large part to play, he would use himself and several others in Cuba whom he could rely upon.
>
> He said he had plans to blow up an oil refinery, as he felt that the continuing existence of a semblance of normal functioning in Cuba depended upon a continuing supply of petroleum, supplies of which, as we know, are at a critical stage today.
>
> He also wanted to plan the execution of Carlos Rodriguez (a top-ranking Castro subordinate) and the Soviet Ambassador, and also to eliminate Fidel, by execution if necessary.
>
> While we were making <u>no</u> commitments or plans, we pointed out to Cubela that schemes like he envisioned certainly had their place, but that a lot of coordination, planning, information-collection, etc., were necessary prerequisites to ensure the value and success of such plans.
>
> Cubela stated that many times during the course of this and subsequent meetings that he was only interested in involving himself in a plan of significant action, and which was truly designed to achieve rapidly his desire to help Cuba.

7-9 August

Because of the security hazard in too frequent meetings in Helsinki, where Cubela was surrounded by his associates in the Cuban delegation, it was agreed that further meetings would be held in Stockholm and in Copenhagen. Cubela agreed to meet with a Spanish-speaking case officer in Paris later in the month. Nothing significant came out of the meetings in Stockholm, 7-9 August, except Cubela's revelation that he had told four of his Cuban associates of his meetings in Helsinki with ▆▆▆▆.

10-11 August 1962

▆▆▆▆, ▆▆▆▆, and Cubela met in Copenhagen for further meetings. ▆▆▆▆ wrote in his contact report:

> ". . . . at one time when we (▆▆▆▆ always wrote of himself as 'we') were discussing the various aspects of Cubela's future role in Cuba, we used the term 'assassinate.' The use of this term, we later learned from ▆▆▆▆ and from Cubela himself, was most objectionable to the latter, and he was visibly upset. It was not the act he objected to, but rather merely the choice of the word used to describe it. 'Eliminate was acceptable'."

(Comment: It is worth noting here that ▆▆▆▆ a Cuban ▆▆▆▆ in New York, was present at a series of meetings at which the assassination of Castro was discussed between Cubela and ▆▆▆▆ whom ▆▆▆▆ knew to be a CIA officer.)

14-23 August 1962

Cubela, ▆▆▆▆ and ▆▆▆▆ met in Paris and were joined by ▆▆▆▆ a Spanish-speaking case officer ▆▆▆▆. Cubela was given S/W training and was issued appropriate S/W supplies. He was taken to the south of France on 20 August for a demolition demonstration. ▆▆▆▆ planned to polygraph Cubela and asked for a polygraph operator to be sent to Paris. Cubela indignantly refused to be polygraphed. ▆▆▆▆ cabled on 17 August:

> "Have no intention give Cubela physical elimination mission as requirement but recognize this something he could or might try to carry out on his own initiative."

Headquarters replied by cable on 18 August:

> "Strongly concur that no physical elimination missions be given Cubela."

29 August 1962

Cubela left Prague by air for Havana.

5-8 September 1963

Cubela attended the Collegiate Games in Porto Alegre, Brazil, as a representative of the Cuban government. He was met there by ▆▆▆▆ and ▆▆▆▆. Also participating was ▆▆▆▆▆▆, a Spanish-speaking case officer from headquarters, who thereafter acted as case officer for Cubela.

Cubela claimed that he had written two S/W messages. (Only one had been received.) He said he was reluctant to use S/W because he feared the efficiency of the Cuban postal censorship.

Cubela discussed a group of Cuban military officers known to him, and possible ways of approaching them. The problem was, he explained, that although many of them were anti-Communist they were either loyal to Fidel or were so afraid of him that they were reluctant to discuss any conspiracies for fear they might be provocations. Cubela said that he thought highly of ▆▆▆▆ (AMTRUNK-▆▆) who was hiding ▆▆▆▆ ▆▆▆▆▆▆▆. ▆▆▆▆ had been sent to Cuba by CIA to recruit ▆▆ in place, and had done so. Cubela said he planned to use ▆▆ but was concerned about ▆▆'s "nervous condition" and the fact that he drank heavily. Cubela was told to assist ▆▆▆ in ▆▆▆▆ intelligence assignments, but not to help ▆▆▆ leave Cuba — as Cubela proposed.

14 September 1963

From Porto Alegre, Cubela flew to Paris, arriving on 14 September. He was there ostensibly to attend the Alliance Francaise, but actually to take an extended vacation — of which he planned to inform Fidel after the fact.

16 September 1963

Cubela (in Paris) wrote to ▆▆▆▆ (in New York): "I don't intend to see (be interviewed by) your friend again," which you should tell them, "so they don't make the trip. I want to get away from politics completely . . ."

3 October 1963

▆▆▆▆▆ arrived in Paris for meetings with Cubela. (The record does not reveal why ▆▆▆▆ went to Paris in the face of Cubela's stated wish not to see him. The letter may have been written during a spell of temporary depression. ▆▆▆▆▆ were already in contact with Cubela when ▆▆▆▆ arrived.) Also participating in the meetings were ▆▆▆▆▆ and ▆▆▆▆▆.

▆▆▆▆▆▆▆▆▆▆▆▆▆▆▆▆▆▆▆▆▆▆▆▆▆
▆▆▆▆▆▆▆▆▆▆▆▆▆▆▆▆▆▆▆▆▆▆▆▆▆
▆▆▆▆▆▆▆▆▆▆▆▆▆▆▆▆▆▆▆▆▆▆▆▆▆
▆▆▆▆▆

11 October 1963

▆▆▆▆ cabled that Cubela was insistent upon meeting with a senior U.S. official, preferably Robert F. Kennedy, for assurances of U.S. moral support for any activity Cubela undertook in Cuba. ▆▆▆▆ said that the answer Cubela received might be crucial to CIA's relationship with Cubela. ▆▆▆▆▆ recommended that "highest and profound consideration be given as feeling drawn by all who in contact Cubela is that he determined attempt op against Castro with or without U.S. support."

13 October 1963

▆▆▆▆▆ cabled: ▆▆ ETA LOND 13 Oct. Pending change after 12 Oct meet ▆▆▆ plans return Hqs after LOND stop in order discuss details operation before entering final round discussions with AMLASH."

17 October 1963

███████ cabled the results of a meeting with Cubela and ███████. Cubela, in a private conversation with ██████, reiterated his desire to speak with a high-level U.S. Government official. ██████ said that basically Cubela wanted assurances that the U.S. Government would support him if his enterprise were successful.

29 October 1963

Desmond FitzGerald, then Chief, SAS, who was going to Paris on other business, arranged to meet with Cubela to give him the assurances he sought. The contact plan for the meeting, a copy of which is in the AMLASH file, has this to say on cover:

> FitzGerald will represent self as personal representative of Robert F. Kennedy who traveled Paris for specific purpose meeting Cubela and giving him assurances of full U.S. support if there is change of the present government in Cuba.

According to FitzGerald, he discussed the planned meeting with the DD/P (Helms) who decided it was not necessary to seek approval from Robert Kennedy for FitzGerald to speak in his name.

The meeting was held in ██████'s house in Paris on 29 October 1963. FitzGerald used the alias ████████ ████████ ████████ acted as interpreter. ████████ was not present during the meeting. ████████████████ on 13 November 1963 wrote a memorandum for the record of the meeting. It reads, in part:

> FitzGerald informed Cubela that the United States is prepared to render all necessary assistance to any anti-communist Cuban group which succeeds in neutralizing the present Cuban leadership and assumes sufficient control to invite the United States to render the assistance it is prepared to give. It was emphasized that the above support will be forthcoming only after a real coup has been effected and the group involved is

in a position to request U.S. (probably under OAS auspices) recognition and support. It was made clear that the U.S. was not prepared to commit itself to supporting an isolated uprising, as such an uprising can be extinguished in a matter of hours if the present government is still in control of Havana. As for the post-coup period, the U.S. does not desire that the political clock be turned back but will support the necessary economic and political reforms which will benefit the mass of the Cuban people.

(Comment: Those involved now recall the purpose of the meeting as being something quite different from that appearing in written records prepared at about the time of the meeting. FitzGerald recalls that Cubela spoke repeatedly of the need for an assassination weapon. In particular, he wanted a high-powered rifle with telescopic sights or some other weapon that could be used to kill Castro from a distance. FitzGerald wanted no part of such a scheme and told ███████ to tell Cubela that the U.S. simply does not do such things. When he was told this, Cubela said he wanted confirmation from a senior U.S. official, not a member of CIA. FitzGerald says that when he met with Cubela in Paris he told Cubela that the U.S. Government would have no part of an attempt on Castro's life. Sam Halpern, who was not present at FitzGerald's meeting with Cubela but who was thoroughly familiar with all that was going on, has a recollection identical with that of FitzGerald.)

Be that as it may, the written record tells a somewhat different story. In ███████ memorandum of the meeting with Cubela he wrote that:

> Nothing of an operational nature was discussed at the FitzGerald meeting. After the meeting Cubela stated that he was satisfied with the policy discussion but now desired to know what technical support we could provide him.

14 November 1963

████ met with ████ in New York City on 14 November. ████'s contact report reveals Cubela's reaction (as told to ████) to his meeting with FitzGerald.

The visit with FitzGerald, who acted in the capacity of a representative of high levels of the Government concerned with the Cuban problem satisfied Cubela as far as policy was concerned, but he was not at all happy with the fact that he still was not given the technical assisstance for the operational plan as he saw it. ████ said that Cubela dwelt constantly on this point. He could not understand why he was denied certain small pieces of equipment which promised a final solution to the problem, while, on the other hand, the U.S. Government gave much equipment and money to exile groups for their ineffective excursions against Cuban coastal targets. According to ████ Cubela feels strongly on this point, and if he does not get advice and materials from a U.S. Government technician, he will probably become fed-up again, and we will lose whatever progress we have made to date.

19 November 1963

Memorandum for the record prepared by ████: "C/SAS (FitzGerald) approved telling Cubela he would be given a cache inside Cuba. Cache could, if he requested it, include . . . high power rifles w/scopes . . . . C/SAS requested written reports on AMLASH operation be kept to a minimum."

20 November 1963

Thus far, this account of the Cubela project has been based almost wholly on documents found in the project file. Beginning here is an account of an episode in the Cubela operation on which there is no documentary evidence. Dr. Gunn has a record of nine contacts and their dates; otherwise, this summary is drawn from the recollections of those involved.

████████ says that, while Cubela was anxious to do away with Castro, Cubela was not willing to sacrifice his own life in exchange for Castro's. What Cubela really wanted was a high-powered, silenced rifle with an effective range of hundreds or thousands of yards. Cubela finally said that, as a doctor of medicine (which he was), he was quite sure that we could devise some technical means of doing the job that would not automatically cause him to lose his own life in the try.

Samuel Halpern and ████████████ approached Dr. Gunn for assistance. Although none of the participants specifically so stated, it may be inferred that they were seeking a means of assassination of a sort that Cubela might reasonably have been expected to have devised himself. What they settled upon was Black Leaf 40, a common, easily-obtainable insecticide containing about 40% nicotine sulphate. Nicotine is a deadly poison that may be administered orally, by injection, or by absorption through the skin. It is likely that there also were discussions of means of administering the poison, because Gunn was ready to move when asked.

The plan reached the action stage when Halpern and ████████ contacted Gunn again on the morning of 20 November 1963 and told him that the device for administering the poison (a ballpoint pen rigged as a hypodermic syringe) had to be ready in time for ████████ to catch a plane at noon the next day. Gunn says that he went immediately to the FI/D workshop and spent the rest of the day and most of that night fabricating the device. Those in FI/D who worked with him knew what he was trying to make but not for whom it was intended. Eventually, after seven or eight failures, he succeeded in converting a Paper-Mate pen into a hypodermic syringe that worked. He said that the needle was so fine that the victim would hardly feel it when it was inserted — he compared it with the scratch from a shirt with too much starch. He delivered the workable device to ████████ the following morning and retained two of the later prototypes. He states that they are still in his safe. He does not know what happened to the device he gave ██████; he does not remember its having been returned to him. He believes he was told that Cubela refused to accept the device. He says he would not now be able to differentiate the final pen from the earlier prototypes that are in his safe.

22 November 1963

██████████ arrived in Paris on the morning of 22 November and met with Cubela late that afternoon. ██████ states that he showed the pen/syringe to Cubela and explained how it worked. He is not sure, but he believes that Cubela accepted the device but said that he would not take it to Cuba with him. ██████ distinctly recalls that Cubela didn't think much of the device. Cubela said that, as a doctor, he knew all about Black Leaf 40 and that we surely could come up with something more sophisticated than that. It should be noted that Gunn and ██████ agree that the syringe was not loaded. Cubela was expected to supply his own poison; we merely suggested Black Leaf 40 as an effective poison for use in the syringe.

██████ wrote a contact report of the meeting. It makes no mention of a pen or of poison. The following is a summary of the contact report. Cubela said that he was returning to Cuba fully determined to pursue his plans to initiate a coup against Castro. ██████ reiterated the assurances given Cubela by FitzGerald of full U.S. support if a real coup against the Castro regime were successful. Cubela asked for the following items to be included in a cache inside Cuba: 20 hand grenades, two high-powered rifles with telescopic sights, and approximately 20 pounds of C-4 explosive and related equipment. Cubela suggested the best place for the cache was on the finca (farm) managed by his friend, ██████████. Since he was returning to Cuba by way of Prague, he did not want to carry S/W or any other incriminating materials with him. As they were coming out of the meeting, ██████ and Cubela were informed that President Kennedy had been assassinated. Cubela was visibly moved over the news. He asked, "Why do such things happen to good people?" The contact report does not state the time nor the duration of the ■■■■■-Cubela meeting, but <u>it is likely that at the very moment President Kennedy was shot a CIA officer was meeting with a Cuban agent in Paris and giving him an assassination device for use against Castro.</u> ■■■■■ states that he received an OPIM cable from FitzGerald that night or early the next morning telling him that everything was off. We do not find such a cable in the AMLASH file. There is a record in the file that ■■■■■ was due to arrive back in Washington at 1810 hours, 23 November.

The AMLASH project was probably about as widely known within the Clandestine Services as any other project of a similar nature. However, we can identify only four people who know of the just-described episode involving a hypodermic syringe and Black Leaf 40. ■■■■■ knew all of the story, Halpern knew most of it, and Gunn knew much of it. FitzGerald did not mention this aspect of the Cubela operation when he first briefed us on it. When we went back to him later with specific questions, he said he remembered something about Black Leaf 40, but nothing whatever about a device for administering it. Gunn said he had the impression that FitzGerald knew about the operation "but didn't want to know." ■■■■■ says that FitzGerald knew that he and Halpern were seeing Gunn. Halpern agrees, but adds that FitzGerald did not know the specifics of the fabricating of an assassination device.

****

Beginning here, the narrative is again drawn from records in the Project AMLASH files.

****

1 December 1963

FBIS reported that Cubela returned to Cuba from Prague.

19 February 1964

The JMWAVE Station reported by cable that two separate, identical caches would be emplaced in support of Project AMLASH during March. One would be put down in Pinar del Rio ▆▆▆▆▆▆▆ ▆▆▆▆. The other would be taken by the AMTRUNKs to the AMTRUNK infiltration area. Each cache would contain, among other things, two FAL 7.62 automatic rifles.

6 March 1964

Cable from the JMWAVE Station: "Unless headquarters has overriding reason unknown WAVE for including FALs in cache to be carried by AMTRUNKs, wish stress following point in WAVE's decision to eliminate FALs: FALs require 7 by 9 by 50 inch oblong cache container which is difficult to handle in the intermediate craft."

7 March 1964

Headquarters replied that: "Reason for desiring include FALs is that this is the main item requested by AMLASH-1."

13 March 1964

The JMWAVE Station cabled: "Since cannot break down FALs to fit available cache container shorter than 50 inches, will omit FALs from AMLASH cache."

17-21 March 1964

The AMLASH cache was put down on Operation AMTRUNK VIII.

24 April 1964

Headquarters cabled ████████████ that ████████████ had been briefed to meet ████████████████, "who has an important message from Cubela."

3 May 1964

████████████████ reported that the message ██████ had from Cubela was that Cubela wanted a silencer for the Belgian FAL submachine gun soonest.

5 May 1964

SAS requested TSD to produce FAL silencers on a crash basis. There are several later documents in the file describing TSD's efforts to silence a FAL and to modify its sights for firing under poor lighting conditions. TSD eventually came up with a silencer ██

████████████████████████████████

9-11 June 1964

████████████ put down an AMLASH cache on the north coast of Pinar del Rio containing, among other things, "two each FAL automatic rifles with five magazines per weapon." No mention is made of silencers. From TSD's reports on development of a silencer, one was not yet ready at the time the cache was prepared.

1 August 1964

The JMWAVE Station reported receipt of an S/W message from ████████████ dated 18 July. It stated that the AMLASH cache put down in the AMTRUNK infiltration area had been located and that steps were being taken to recover its contents. The message said that it was hoped the cache contained "two high-powered rifles with silencers," because ██████████ was not yet certain that he could recover the cache put down in Pinar del Rio by ████████████.

30 August 1964

Manuel Artime received information through Madrid that a group of dissident members of the Castro regime desired to establish direct contact with Artime. On 7 October 1964, an Artime associate went to France for a meeting with an intermediary from the dissident group. The intermediary was named as Alberto BLANCO Romariz.

12 November 1964

FBIS report: "A delegation of the University Student Federation of Cuba arrived in Prague on 11 November to participate in the meeting of the Executive Council of the International Student Union to be held from 14 to 17 November. The delegation is made up of . . . Maj. Rolando Cubela, who will attend the event as a special guest of the IUS."

13 November 1964

Contact report of a meeting in Washington with Artime: "Artime agreed to talk to AMLASH-1 if it turns out that he is the contact man for the internal dissident group. Artime thinks that if AMLASH-1 is the chief of the dissident group we can all forget about the operation."

25 November 1964

█████████████ reported Cubela's arrival in Paris.

4 December 1964

█████████████ prepared a memorandum request for $6,500 as an extraordinary budget expenditure for the travel of Artime for maintaining contact with the internal dissident group's representatives in Europe during November and December 1964. There is no direct indication in the file that the request was approved, but indirect evidence indicates that it was. Artime did travel to Europe and maintained the contacts.

6-7 December 1964

████████ met Cubela in Paris. This is a summary of the details reported by ████████. Cubela, although unhappy because he was unable to carry out his plans during the past year, continued to feel that his solution to the Cuban problem was the only one feasible and that he had to continue trying. Cubela was told that the U.S. Government could not and would not in any way become involved or provide assistance in the task he had planned for himself. Cubela appeared to understand our position and said that if he needed help he would look elsewhere.

10 December 1964

Memorandum prepared by Sanchez and left with ████████, of the ████████ as background on the then current status of the AMLASH operation — excerpts:

> "Artime does not know, and we do not plan to tell him that we are in direct contact with Cubela, ████████████████████████ ████████████████████
>
> "Cubela was told and fully understands that U.S. Government cannot become involved to any degree in the 'first step' of his plan. If he needs support, he realizes that he will have to get it elsewhere. FYI: This is where Artime could fit in nicely in giving any support Cubela would request."
>
> (Comment: Sanchez explained to us that what had happened was that SAS contrived to put Artime and Cubela together in such a way that neither knew that the contact had been engineered by CIA. The thought was that Artime needed a man inside and Cubela wanted a silenced weapon, which CIA was unwilling to furnish to him directly. By putting the two together, Artime might get his man inside and Cubela might get his silenced weapon — from Artime. CIA did not intend to furnish an assassination weapon for Artime to give to Cubela, and did not do so.)

1 December 1964

Headquarters cable to Paris: "When ██████ contacts Cubela to debrief him, . . . please confirm statement by Cubela to ██████ that only money and a few commo items were retrieved by the fishermen. Cubela and ██████ unhappy that fishermen had not recovered more from the cache, but it was not possible for Cubela and ██████ to go to the site of the cache personally. (Cubela had told ██████ that ██████ had used some "fishermen" to recover the cache and that not all of it was recovered. This was the cache put down in the AMTRUNK infiltration area, which did not include the FAL rifles.)

27 December 1964

Artime and Cubela met for the first time — in Madrid.

30 December 1964

Artime and Cubela met for a second time in Madrid on 30 December. Artime reported the results in a meeting with ██████ in Florida on 3 January 1965. Cubela told Artime that he had requested a silencer for a FAL rifle from the Americans, which they had not been able to provide. Artime agreed to furnish either a silencer for a FAL or a comparable rifle with silencer. If Artime obtained a silencer for a FAL, Cubela would personally carry it back to Cuba with him. If Artime had to settle for some other type of silenced rifle, he would cache it in Cuba for Cubela.

28 January 1965

██████ arrived in Paris for meetings with Cubela.

2 February 1965

██████ cabled from Paris: "Cubela and ██████ returned Paris 31 January. Met 1 February. Cubela states full agreement reached with Artime and he well satisfied with arrangements which he outlined

for our information (along same lines as reported by Artime). . . .
Artime providing package in Madrid which Cubela plans carry
back in personal luggage."

⬛⬛⬛ cabled from Paris: "As of November 1964 when Cubela
departed Cuba neither he nor ⬛⬛⬛ had received any part of the
Matanzas cache. ⬛⬛⬛ told him fishermen recovered money
and parts of communications gear but that money was no good
since it was in a series out of circulation."

11 February 1965

⬛⬛⬛ cabled: "From Cubela on 10 February: On 10 or 11
February Cubela is to receive one pistol with silencer and one
Belgian FAL rifle with silencer from Artime's secretary. Both
weapons come from U.S. and now in Madrid." (This is in conflict
with the earlier report that Artime would cache a rifle and silencer
if that were all he could find. We are unable to resolve the conflict.)

12 February 1965

⬛⬛⬛ cabled: "Artime reported on final meeting
with Cubela: Artime had three packages of special items made up
by his technical people and delivered to Cubela in Madrid. Cubela
seemed satisfied."

4 March 1965

⬛⬛⬛ reported receiving a telephone call from a friend in
Havana who had seen Cubela back in Havana the previous day.

15 March 1965

⬛⬛⬛ cabled that one Rafael GARCIA-BANGO Dirube
had arrived in Madrid from Cuba on 15 March and had been
introduced ⬛⬛⬛ claimed to be in contact
with a group of Cuban military leaders who were planning to
eliminate Castro and take over the government. It quickly became

clear that he was referring to Cubela. ▮▮▮▮▮▮▮▮ said that he had always been publicly identified as a close friend of Cubela, whom he last saw in Havana on 9 March. ▮▮▮▮▮▮▮▮ said that he had been the lawyer ▮▮▮▮▮▮▮▮▮▮▮▮▮▮▮▮▮▮▮▮▮▮▮▮

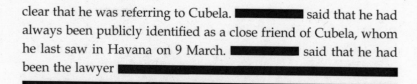

(Comment: This is another name-link between Cubela and the gambling syndicate plots reported upon earlier in this report. ▮▮▮▮▮▮▮▮ was one of the principals in Shef Edwards' Phase One of the operation. He presumably was not involved in Phase Two under Harvey, but we cannot be sure of that. After all, ▮▮▮▮▮▮▮▮ was the man who brought Varona into the operation late in Phase One, and Varona was one of the main players during Phase Two. The three-man team that was sent in by Varona was reported on 21 June 1962 to be in place in Cuba.)

June 1965

Headquarters decided to terminate all contacts with key members of the Cubela group. It had become increasingly apparent that the circle of Cubans who knew of Cubela's plans and of CIA's association with them was ever-widening. The last straw came early in June 1965. (Note: There is a discrepancy in dates. The memorandum prepared at the time lists dates of 2, 3, and 4 May. From other evidence in the file, it is apparent that the month was June — not May.) One ▮▮▮▮▮▮▮▮▮▮▮▮, a former PM trainee who was terminated as a malcontent on 20 March 1961, contacted an I&NS agent on 2 June 1965 with a story that ▮▮▮▮▮ thought affected U.S. security. I&NS heard him out and then sent him to the FBI. The FBI listened to the story on 3 June and then sent him to CIA. A CIA officer interviewed him on 4 June. ▮▮▮▮▮▮ said that in May he had received a letter from a friend in Paris urging him to meet in Paris with a friend of Cubela. ▮▮▮▮▮▮ went to Paris and met with ▮▮▮▮▮▮▮▮ one of Cubela's closest associates in the supposed plan to assassinate Castro. ▮▮▮▮▮▮ claimed to have a message from Cubela, which Cubela wanted ▮▮▮▮▮ to deliver to CIA. The message was that Cubela and the others with him were in a position to kill Castro and others in the regime, but they needed some help and to know whether the CIA and the U.S. Government were with them and willing to support them. If the answer were affirmative, Cubela would send out details on what he needed. From his story it was obvious that ▮▮▮▮▮ knew the full details of the Cubela operation.

(Comment: There is no indication in the file that CIA ever found out the sort of "help" Cubela thought he needed. At a meeting in Paris on 1 February 1965 he asked for $10,000 "to organize the internal group." CIA refused to give him the money and suggested he try to get it from Artime. Cubela was quite upset over the turn down. A few days later, in Madrid, he approached a Cuban ▮▮▮▮▮▮▮▮▮▮, claiming he was stranded in Madrid with no money. Headquarters approved a "personal loan" of $200. On 16 February 1965, Cubela asked ▮▮▮▮▮ for $1,000, which headquarters approved giving him. In a later meeting with ▮▮▮▮▮▮ in New York City, ▮▮▮▮▮ said that he had given Cubela $7,000.)

On 23 June 1965 headquarters sent a cable to the stations concerned directing termination of contact with members of the Cubela group. It read, in part:

". . . convincing proof that entire AMLASH group insecure and that further contact with key members of group constitutes menace to CIA operations against Cuba as well as to the security of CIA staff personnel in Western Europe.

"Under the circumstances headquarters desires that contact with key members of the group be eliminated as rapidly as possible, and that assets who may be in contact with individual members of the group or peripherally involved in AMLASH conspiracy be warned of danger implicit in these associations and directed to eliminate contacts ASAP."

1 March 1966

Reuters reported from Havana that the Cuban security police had arrested two military officers for alleged counterrevolutionary activities involving the U.S. Central Intelligence Agency. They were identified as Maj. Rolando Cubela and Maj. Ramon Guin.

7 March 1966

FBIS quoting Havana Domestic Service: "The trial of the accused Rolando Cubela, Ramon Guin, and others who are linked to the U.S. Central Intelligence Agency, was begun in the revolutionary court of Havana district in La Cabana today at 1500 hours."

8 March 1966

Excerpts from first day's trial proceedings as reported by the Havana Domestic Service and copied by FBIS:

> Former Majors Rolando Cubela and Ramon Guin as well as others who are under indictment have confessed their guilt. The defendants are being tried for crimes against the integrity and stability of the nation by having planned the assassination of Maj. Fidel Castro.
>
> The defendants are Rolando Cubela Secades, Ramon Guin Diaz, Jose Luis Gonzalez Gallarreta, Alberto Blanco Romariz, and Juan Alsina Navarro, all of whom confessed their guilt in the imputed facts of the case. Also appearing in the trial were Guillermo Cunill Alvarez and Angel Herrero Veliz.
>
> The accused Jose Luis Gonzales Gallarreta, who worked as diplomatic attache in the Cuban Embassy in Spain, betrayed his country for 100,000 dollars given him by CIA agents whom he contacted only a month after his arrival in Spain. (He) met with an official of the aforementioned organization of international subversion named James Noel who covered his activities by appearing as an official of the U.S. Embassy in Spain. Noel demanded that biographic information and information about

the Cuban diplomatic mission be furnished him under this arrangement.

Cubela during his stay in Europe makes three trips to Spain, on 26 December 1964, and on 6 and 20 February 1965. The revolutionary ringleader Artime goes to Madrid at the beginning of February 1965. A meeting is held between Cubela and Artime in which they agree on the final plan.

This plan would begin with a personal attack aimed at Maj. Fidel Castro Ruz. This criminal act would be followed by an armed invasion of the country 48 hours later by U.S. troops. The attack against Comrade Fidel Castro would be made using a 7.62mm FAL rifle that Cubela owned. This weapon would be fitted with a powerful 4x40 telescopic sight and a silencer.

Artime sent Gallego to the United States to get the telescopic sight and the silencer. Once obtained, this equipment was delivered to Blanco Romariz. He in turn delivered it to Gonzalez Gallarreta who then delivered it to Cubela the day before he left Madrid.

In order to insure the success of his plans, Cubela meets with defendant Guin. Guin had been recruited since September 1963 as a spy for the Yankee CIA. This recruiting was done by CIA agent Miguel Diaz who infiltrated Cuba in order to recruit him, and did so.

Seized in Cubela's residence was a Tasco brand telescopic sight with accessories, the FAL rifle, large quatities of weapons and ammunition for them, fragmentation and incendiary grenades, and other military equipment and materiel.

The punishment to which the defendants are subject and which this prosecution wishes imposed is as follows: For Rolando Cubela Secades, Ramon Guin Diaz, Jose Luis Gonzalez Gallarreta, and Alberto Blanco Romariz — the death penalty by firing squad. For Juan Alsina Navarro, Guillermo Cunill Alvarez and Angel Herrero Veliz — 30 years imprisonment plus corresponding additional penalties.

9 March 1966

FBIS report from Havana Domestic Service: "Prime Minister Fidel Castro has sent a letter to the prosecutor in the case . . . against Majors Rolando Cubela, Ramon Guin, and other defendants. In it, the Prime Minister says that it must be recognized from all this, a bitter but useful lesson may be drawn, adding, 'I suggest that the court not ask the death sentence for any of the accused'."

10 March 1966

FBIS report of testimony given in court on 8 March:

Question: Do you recall when the silencer broke?

Cubela: The silencer? Actually, the silencer did not break. The silencer actually did not break.

Question: Where is the silencer?

Cubela: I threw the silencer away because it was burning my hands.

Prosecutor: Have you spoken with Comrade Fidel Castro recently?

Cubela: Yes.

Prosecutor: Can you tell the court when you spoke with Comrade Fidel?

Cubela: I believe it was in January, let me see, in January, in January.

Prosecutor: In January! Do you recall the conversation you had with Comrade Fidel, and did Comrade Fidel offer to help you?

Cubela: Comrade Fidel opened the doors, opened the doors to me. He gave me, he gave me to understand that he knew what I was doing but I did not have enough courage to tell him.

****

Defense Attorney: Cubela Secades, what, in your view, is the punishment merited by conduct of this nature?

Cubela: The worst!

Question: What do you mean by "the worst?"
Cubela: The wall.
Question: What do you mean by "the wall?"
Cubela: Deserved execution by a firing squad.

11 March 1966

FBIS report quoting Havana Domestic Service of 10 March:

Revolutionary Court No. 1, which has tried case 108 in crimes against the integrity and security of the nation, has pronounced sentences on the accused Rolando Cubela Secades, Ramon Guin Diaz, and others.

According to the sentences, Rolando Cubela and Ramon Guin were sentenced to 25 years imprisonment; Jose Luis Gonzalez Gallarreta and Alberto Blanco Romariz, 20 years; and Juan Hilario Alsina Navarro, 10 years.

Guillermo Cunill Alvarez and Angel Harrero Veliz were absolved of guilt. They were released provided they are not liable to any other charges.

(Comment: It is worth noting that none of Cubela's dealings with CIA from March 1961 until November 1964 were mentioned in the trial proceedings. The first association of Cubela with CIA was in connection with his trip to Europe in late 1964 and early 1965 during which he had his meetings with Artime. The trial evidence was confined to Cubela's counterrevolutionary activities growing out of those meetings with Artime in December 1964 and February 1965. None of his many direct contacts with CIA officers, some of whom he knew by true name, were mentioned. There is not even a hint of the ballpoint pen/hypodermic/Black Leaf 40 episode. The Cuban authorities may have gotten that information from him and decided not to introduce it in evidence, but we can think of no convincing reason why they would have withheld it. The closest we can come to a decent reason, and it is pure conjecture, is this: Castro may have thought it politically imprudent to allow the execution of someone so close to his inner circle, who had merely plotted without acting. If the full details of Cubela's involvement with CIA had come out in court, Castro might have had little excuse for asking for leniency.)

Discussion of Assassination at High-Level Government Meetings

Drew Pearson claims to have a report that there was a high-level meeting at the Department of State at which plans for the assassination of Castro were discussed. We find record of two high-level, interagency meetings at which assassination of Castro was raised. The first (and probably the one to which Pearson refers) was at the Department of State on 10 August 1962. It was a meeting of the Special Group (Augmented). The second meeting we have identified was held on 30 July 1964. It was a meeting of the 303 Committee and probably was held in the White House Situation Room. The two meetings are described separately below.

10 August 1962

The Special Group (Augmented) met at the Department of State, either in Secretary Rusk's office or in his conference room. The following are recorded as being present:

State:	Dean Rusk, Alexis Johnson, Edwin Martin, Richard Goodwin, Robert Hurwitch
White House:	Maxwell Taylor, McGeorge Bundy (Bill Harvey's notes record that Robert Kennedy was absent and that Bundy had his proxy.)
Defense:	Robert McNamara, Roswell Gilpatric, Lyman Lemnitzer, Edward Lansdale

CIA:	John McCone, William Harvey
USIA:	Edward Murrow, Donald Wilson
Secretary:	Thomas Parrott

Tom Parrott's minutes of the meeting make no mention of the subject of assassination. Both McCone and Harvey recall that McNamara raised the subject. Harvey's notes taken at the meeting show that it was also mentioned by Murrow, but the nature of the comments was not recorded. Mr. McCone states, in a memorandum of 14 April 1967, that he recalls meetings on 8 or 9 August in the JCS Operations Room in the Pentagon and on 10 August 1962 in Secretary Rusk's conference room. At one of these meetings (and McCone now recalls it as being at the JCS) the suggestion was made that top people in the Cuban regime, including Castro, be liquidated.

(Comment: As it will later be seen, Mr. McCone's recollection is probably faulty. It is quite clear that assassination came up for discussion at the 10 August meeting at State.)

Mr. McCone says that he took immediate exception to the discussion and promptly after the meeting called on Secretary McNamara personally to emphasize his position. According to McCone, McNamara "heartily agreed." McCone states in his memorandum that at no time did the suggestion receive serious consideration by the Special Group (Augmented) or by any individual responsible for policy. McCone adds that through the years the Cuban problem was discussed in terms such as "dispose of Castro," "remove Castro," and "knock off Castro," etc., but that these phrases were always construed to mean the overthrowing of the communist government in Cuba. Harvey recalls that, when McCone told him of the McCone-McNamara conversation, McCone said that if he, McCone, were to be involved in such a thing he would be excommunicated.

Following the 10 August meeting, and without reference to the reported exchange between McCone and McNamara, Lansdale addressed a memorandum on 13 August to William Harvey (CIA), Robert Hurwitch (State), General Harris (Defense), and Don Wilson (USIA). The memorandum assigned responsibility for drafting papers on various subjects related to the Cuban operation. Harvey's assignment included: "Intelligence, Political (splitting the regime, [portion excised from the CIA file copy])."

On 14 August, Harvey submitted a memorandum to the DD/P (Helms) reporting the Lansdale communication and what Harvey had done about it. Harvey's memorandum to the DD/P states that the excised portion had consisted of the phrase: "including elimination of leaders". Harvey wrote that he had phoned Lansdale's office and had spoken with Frank Hand in Lansdale's absence. Harvey said he had protested the use of the phrase and had proposed that steps be taken to have it excised from all copies. This was agreed to. Harvey deleted the phrase from his own copy and assumes that instructions were given to other recipients to do the same. Harvey told us that Lansdale repeatedly tried to raise the matter of assassination of Castro with Harvey over the next several weeks. Harvey says that he always avoided such discussions. Harvey estimates that five persons in Lansdale's office were generally aware of the sensitive details of Project MONGOOSE and of Lansdale's interest in assassination as an aspect of it.

30 July 1964

The 303 Committee met in regular session, probably in the Situation Room of the White House. (Desmond FitzGerald recalls that such meetings were generally held there.) The following are recorded as being present:

McGeorge Bundy, Cyrus Vance, John McCone, Thomas Hughes

Desmond FitzGerald for the discussion on Cuba

Col. Ralph Steakley was present for another item on the agency, but it is not shown if he was present when the Cuba item was discussed.

Peter Jessup as secretary.

The minutes of the meeting record this in the context of the discussion of Cuba:

> "It was agreed that Mr. FitzGerald would contact Mr. Sam Papich of the FBI in regard to the earlier report of an alleged plot with Mafia overtones to assassinate Castro and which the Attorney General agreed to handle as a matter of law enforcement."

The reference is clearly to a 10 June 1964 memorandum information report from DD/P to the Director. The following additional "elite" dissemination was made of it:

Special Assistant to the President for National Security Affairs
Assistant Secretary, Inter-American Affairs, Department of State
Director of Intelligence and Research, Department of State
Director, Defense Intelligence Agency
The Attorney General
Director, Federal Bureau of Investigation
Deputy Director of Central Intelligence
Deputy Director for Intelligence

The report related a proposal for the assassination of Castro that was made to prominent Cuban exiles. The Mafia appeared to be involved in the scheme. The asking price for doing the job was $150,000, with a guarantee of $10,000 for expenses. A wealthy Cuban exile, ████████████████████████████ ████████████ was reported ready to contribute $50,000. ████ approached the Chief of Station, JMWAVE, and suggested that the U.S. Government also contribute funds. The suggestion was rejected out of hand. The record indicates that CIA's only involvement in the plot was to report information of its existence. The last record we find of the incident is a memorandum from the DCI (McCone) to Bundy, dated 19 August 1964, reporting the results of FBI interviews with the alleged participants. Obviously nothing came of the plot.

> (Comment: It may be only coincidence, but we are struck by the point that this group of plotters, allegedly including gangster elements, offered to assassinate Castro for $150,000, which is precisely the sum that CIA offered to pay in an earlier plot that very definitely involved gangster elements. It could be the same group of gangsters, or it could be that the criminal underworld knows the "going price.")

As we have said earlier, if Drew Pearson has firm information on a high-level meeting at which assassination of Castro was discussed, it is likely that the reference would be to the 10 August 1962 meeting of the Special Group (Augmented). The 30 July 1964 303 Committee Meeting is described only because its reference to assassination of Castro might be distorted to assume some of the characteristics of the Pearson story.

The Drew Pearson Story

Published Details	The Facts As We Know Them
The CIA hatched a plot to knock off Castro.	*True.*
Robert Kennedy may have approved an assassination plot.	*Not true. He was briefed on Gambling Syndicate-Phase One after it was over. He was not briefed on Phase Two.*

Underworld figures were actually recruited to carry out the plot.

True.

Three hired assassins were caught in Havana where a lone survivor is still supposed to be languishing in prison.

Roselli informed Harvey on 21 June 1962, presumably on the basis of information from Varona, that a team of three men was inside Cuba. We do not know their identities nor what may have happened to them. We have no proof that they were actually dispatched. None of the announced captures and executions during this period fits this team.

Castro learned enough at least to believe the CIA was seeking to kill him. He is reported to have cooked up a counterplot against President Kennedy.

This reportedly has come out in the Garrison investigations. It was also stated by Castillo in the Philippines under direct interrogation. We have no independent confirmation of any sort. (Note that Garrison met with Roselli in Las Vegas in March 1967.)

Unpublished Details

Pills were sent to Cuba for use in the assassination.

True. At least we were told by Roselli that the pills were sent in during Phase One and again in Phase Two.

There was a meeting at the Department of State at which the assassination of Castro was discussed.

True. The subject was raised at a meeting at State on 10 August 1962, but it is unrelated to any actual attempts at assassination. It did result in a MONGOOSE action memorandum by Lansdale assigning to CIA action for planning liquidation of leaders. The offending phrase was later excised from copies forwarded to CIA, State, Defense, and USIA, but the damage may already have been done.

The Possible Ramifications of the Gambling Syndicate Operation

The earlier sections of this report describe all of the CIA schemes aimed at the assassination of Castro that we have been able to discover. The accounts of the two phases of the gambling syndicate operations are factual to the extent that they are based on what those interviewed recall or believe the facts to have been. It is evident that some of those facts have leaked, are being talked about, or are being peddled. On the opposite page is a list of the main details of the story Drew Pearson has, as they are known to us, together with a brief comment on the apparent accuracy of each. There is support in fact for most of the details in Pearson's story. He has a garbled account of the role played by Robert Kennedy, and he errs in telling the story as if all of the details are part of a single story, which they are not. For the most part, though, his facts are straight and he has the truly important aspects of the gambling syndicate operation.

Until James O'Connell returned on 2 May from his meetings in Las Vegas, we were faced with the difficulty of being unable to estimate the dimensions of the problem facing the Agency unless we could discover what has been leaked, by whom, to whom, and for what purpose. None of those things could be deduced with confidence from the information then available to us. O'Connell, who has already reported to you orally and will be submitting his written report directly to you, is able to shed some light on the likely sources of Pearson's information. He has also briefed us on his conversations with Maheu. These are the key points:

a. Maheu did brief his attorney, Edward P. Morgan, on Maheu's participation in Phase One.

b. Maheu knew nothing of Phase Two while it was under way and has never heard of it from Roselli.

c. Morgan and Roselli were acquainted, independently of Maheu, well before Maheu became involved with Roselli in the gambling syndicate operation. Roselli was steered to Morgan by H.M. Greenspun, editor and publisher of the *Las Vegas Sun*.

d. Maheu suspects that Roselli is a client of Morgan's.

e. Roselli is drinking heavily. Morgan has been in Las Vegas once or twice recently, was drinking too much, and was "indiscreet."

f. Jim Garrison, Edward Morgan, and Roselli were all in Las Vegas at the same time this past March. Garrison was in touch with Roselli; so was Morgan. It is our impression that Greenspun was also involved in the conversations. We do not know the date, but it might be noted that one of Pearson's columns appeared on 7 March.

g. According to Maheu, Morgan and Jack Anderson, Drew Pearson's associate, are very close.

This seems clearly to point the finger at Roselli as the ultimate source of the information on the gambling syndicate plot and to confirm Morgan as Pearson's source.

We can test the accuracy of this assumption against analysis we had done earlier in an effort to identify the likely source of Pearson's story. On the opposite page is a listing of persons definitely known to be witting of certain key facts now in Pearson's possession. The list includes CIA officers who knew more than one of the key facts, plus all known outsiders. These were our conclusions:

a. If Drew Pearson has a single source, and if Pearson's immediate source is the ultimate source of the leak, and if compartmentation was not violated, then Bill Harvey emerges as the likely candidate. He was the only person we

Lethal Pills	Briefing of Kennedy*	Three-Man Team	State Dept. Meeting
Harvey	Harvey	Harvey	Harvey
Roselli	Roselli	Roselli	
Maheu	Maheu		
O'Connell	O'Connell		
Edwards	Edwards		
Houston	Houston		
Varona		Varona	
Varona's son-in-law		Varona's son-in-law	
Maceo		Maceo	
Giancana			
Trafficante			
Orta			

* It is quite possible that the fact of Robert Kennedy's having been briefed, and perhaps the substance of the briefing, is more widely known to government officials than this list would indicate. We know that Mr. McCone on 16 August 1963 asked for and received a copy of the memorandum record of the briefing. Others in Justice and the FBI besides Kennedy may know of the memorandum and of its contents.

found in the course of this inquiry who knew all four of the key facts at the time the Pearson columns appeared. We preferred not to think that Bill Harvey was the culprit. We could find no persuasive reason why he would wish to leak the story deliberately, and we doubted that he would be so indiscreet as to leak it accidentally. Further, if he were the source, we could expect Pearson's story to be completely accurate, because Harvey knew the truth.

b. If we ruled out Harvey as the source, then it appeared that there must be at least two ultimate sources of leaks. The State Department meeting was not known to any of the other participants in the operation — assuming that Harvey did not mention it to any of them. Therefore, it is quite possible that the leak on the State Department meeting has come from someone who has no direct knowledge of the gambling syndicate operation but does know of the meeting.

c. From the standpoint of who-knew-what, the next most likely source of the original leak is John Roselli. He is, in fact, the only person with direct and continuous participation throughout both phases of the gambling syndicate operation. He introduced Maheu to Sam Giancana as the first step in getting the operation under way, and he was the one who made the final break with Varona when the operation was abandoned. He knows everything that went on with the gangsters, with Orta, and with Varona between those dates. He and Robert Maheu are the only non-CIA participants with immediate knowledge of the Robert Kennedy aspect. Shef Edwards had lunch with Roselli and Maheu in Los Angeles in the summer of 1962. Edwards says that Roselli knew Edwards' true name and his position in the Agency. Edwards said he took the occasion to express his personal appreciation to Roselli, and told Roselli that he, Edwards, had personally told Attorney General Kennedy of what Roselli had tried to do in the national interest. We know that Kennedy was merely briefed on the operation — and only on Phase One at that — but Roselli may have inferred that Kennedy had an active role in the operation.

d. We did not know what Robert Maheu knew of the operation firsthand, because we had conflicting information on precisely when he was cut off from direct participation. He has direct knowledge of the first phase, but probably little if any of the second phase (from which Pearson's story seems to come). If Maheu knows of the second phase, he could have learned of it only from Roselli.

e. Maceo, about whom we know very little, was "Roselli's man" in the second phase. He presumably knows of the pills and of the three-man team, but the other details he could have known only from Roselli.

f. Varona's knowledge and that of his son-in-law would be limited to the pills and the team, but they should know considerably more of the specifics; such as, who received the pills, the composition of the team, and the eventual fate of the team.

g. Giancana and Trafficante were presumably cut out of Phase Two. They could have learned of it only from Roselli.

About all that emerged from this review of "who had direct knowledge of what" was support for the hypothesis that Drew Pearson's story probably is drawn from more than one informant: one on the State Department meeting and another (or others) on the gambling syndicate operation. We also postulated that Roselli is the most likely ultimate source of Pearson's story. This line of reasoning and the information O'Connell got from Maheu are consistent.

Our supposition until now was that the immediate and the ultimate sources, if different people, were leaking or peddling the story with ulterior motives in mind. What those ulterior motives might be were difficult to fathom — for these reasons:

a. If protection was what the source was seeking, he could be better assured of getting it by a direct approach to CIA for help.

b. Maheu was the only known link associating Morgan with the syndicate plot, and Maheu stands only to lose by having his role become common knowledge.

c. Those who know Morgan, Maheu, and Roselli thought it quite out of character for any of the three to be spreading the story deliberately for a private purpose.

In learning of the Roselli-Morgan link, we are relieved of the need for speculation as to how the story has gotten out. It is quite likely that Roselli is the source, Morgan the channel, and Anderson and Pearson the recipients. We may also be relieved of the need for speculation as to why the story is being told. The inference to be drawn from O'Connell's discoveries in Las Vegas is that Roselli is drinking too much and talking and that Morgan is also drinking and talking to a newspaperman friend.

Put in its best light — that there is no ulterior motive in spreading the story — it is questionable whether we are any better off now than we were before; our position may be even worse than we had suspected.

a. We may now assume that Pearson's story is not patched together from bits and pieces picked up here and there. His ultimate source, Roselli, knows more about certain details of the gambling syndicate operation than we do, and he evidently has talked. Trying now to hush up further leaks might do more harm than good; the story is already out and probably in considerable detail.

b. The Roselli-Garrison contact in Las Vegas in March is particularly disturbing. It lends substance to reports that Castro had something to do with the Kennedy assassination in retaliation for U.S. attempt on Castro's life. We do not know that Castro actually tried to retaliate, but we do know that there were such plots against Castro. Unhappily, it now appears that Garrison may also know this.

The publicity on this subject has probably not yet run its course.

a. Drew Pearson has not yet, as far as we know, used two of his best goodies: the story of the pills and the fact of the State Department meeting.

b. Garrison has not yet revealed his full case. When he does, we should expect to find CIA prominently displayed.

c. The Philippine National Bureau of Investigation has a Puerto Rican in custody who claims he participated in a Castro-inspired assassination plot in Dallas. He also claims that Castro made a speech in July 1962 threatening to try to assassinate Kennedy in retaliation for two Kennedy attempts on Castro's life. (We have found no record nor recollection of Castro having made such a speech.) The Puerto Rican is in the Philippines illegally and probably will be deported to U.S. We may expect the FBI to take him over and wring him dry.

We face the likelihood that things will get worse before they begin to get better. In the following paragraphs we explore some of the ramifications and discuss what might be done about them.

Should we try to silence those who are talking or might later talk?
It appears to us that this tactic offers little chance of success. For one thing, the story is already out and probably in about as full detail as it ever will be. The only participant on whom we have any real leverage is Maheu, and he has already done all of the talking he is likely to do (to his lawyer, Morgan). We have no hold on any of the others who might furnish confirmation for Roselli's story.

a. Varona is almost certainly not a friend of the Agency. As the Bay of Pigs operation developed, Varona was one of the most critical of the lack of Cuban control of the operation and of the people involved in it. He was bitter over termination of Agency support of his exile group (and the consequent loss of his own income). The last we know of him he was in New York living a hand-to-mouth existence as a part-time auto salesman.

b. Roselli, Giancana, and Trafficante have fallen on "evil" days. Giancana is reported (in a Chicago newspaper of recent date) to have been deposed as the Mafia head in Chicago and was rumored to be hiding in Mexico. Maheu reports that Trafficante is in jail in Tampa. Roselli is persona non grata in Las Vegas, being required to register with the police any time he is town. None of them would have compunctions about dragging in his CIA connection when he was being pushed by law enforcement authorities. Giancana has already done it when the FBI was crowding him in 1963. Roselli appears to be doing it in his conversations with Morgan and Garrison.

(Comment: The cover story used with Roselli, Giancana, Trafficante, Varona, and presumably with Orta was that the sponsors were U.S. businessmen with interests in Cuba. Roselli soon concluded that CIA was the true sponsor and so told O'Connell. In Roselli's subsequent dealings with Harvey and Edwards he came to know this for sure. Giancana named CIA in 1963. We must assume that the others, with the possible exception of Orta and perhaps Varona, are equally sure that CIA was the true sponsor.)

c. Morgan may always retire behind the screen of an attorney-client relationship, as he reportedly did when the FBI approached him on the Pearson story.

d. Pearson, Anderson, and Greenspun (in Las Vegas) are newspapermen with a newsworthy story. Pearson has already published much of it.

e. Maheu does have good reason for not wanting the story aired further. Unfavorable publicity might cause him to lose his lucrative client, Howard Hughes. There might be some value to be gained from endorsing his suggestion that he approach Morgan and perhaps Roselli and urge discretion.

What do other components of Government know about this operation?

Former Attorney General Robert Kennedy was fully briefed by Houston and Edwards on 7 May 1962. A memorandum confirming the oral briefing was forwarded to Kennedy on 14 May 1962. The memorandum does not use the word "assassinate," but there is little room for misinterpretation of what was meant. Presumably the original of that memorandum is still in the files of the Justice Department. It should be noted that the briefing of Kennedy was restricted to Phase One of the operation, which had ended about a year earlier. Phase Two was already under way at the time of the briefing, but Kennedy was not told of it.

As far as we know, the FBI has not been told the sensitive operational details, but it would be naive to assume that they have not by now put two and two together and come out with the right answer. They know of CIA's involvement with Roselli and Giancana as a result of the Las Vegas wiretapping incident. From the Chicago newspaper stories of August 1963, and from Giancana's own statement, it appears that they know this related to Cuba. When Roselli's story reached them (Roselli to Morgan to Pearson to Warren to Rowley to the FBI), all of the pieces should have fallen into place. They should by now have concluded that CIA plotted the assassination of Castro and used U.S. gangster elements in the operation.

There is some support for this thesis in the conversation I had with Sam Papich on 3 May 1967 when I told him of the expected meeting between Roselli and Harvey. Sam commented that Roselli and Giancana have CIA "over a barrel" because of "that operation." He said that he doubted that the FBI would be able to do anything about either Roselli or Giancana because of "their previous activities with your people."

Can we plausibly deny that we plotted with gangster elements to assassinate Castro?

No, we cannot. We are reasonably confident that there is nothing in writing outside of the Government that would confirm Pearson's story of the gambling syndicate operation, but there are plenty of non-gangster witnesses who could lend confirmation.

> a. Maheu can confirm that Shef Edwards told Roselli that Edwards had told the Attoney General of Roselli's activities on behalf of the Government.
>
> b. Varona and Varona's son-in-law can confirm the pill and three-man team elements of the story.
>
> c. Orta can confirm the pill element of Phase One.
>
> d. If an independent investigation were to be ordered, the investigators could learn everything that we have learned. Such an investigation probably would uncover details unknown to us, because it would have access to the non-CIA participants.

Can CIA state or imply that it was merely an instrument of policy?

Not in this case. While it is true that Phase Two was carried out in an atmosphere of intense Kennedy administration pressure to do something about Castro, such is not true of the earlier phase. Phase One was initiated in August 1960 under the Eisenhower administration. Phase Two is associated in Harvey's mind with the Executive Action Capability, which reportedly was developed in response to White House urgings. Again, Phase One had been started and abandoned months before the Executive Action Capability appeared on the scene.

When Robert Kennedy was briefed on Phase One in May 1962, he strongly admonished Houston and Edwards to check with the Attorney General in advance of any future intended use of U.S. criminal elements. This was not done with respect to Phase Two, which was already well under way at the time Kennedy was briefed. The Pearson story, which is now causing us so much distress, includes one detail that is found only in Phase Two: the three-man team.

What measures might be taken to lessen the damage?

We see little to be gained from personal approaches now to Maheu, Morgan, or Roselli. Maheu has much to lose and might be able to prevail upon Morgan and Roselli not to spread the story further. It is questionable whether any such urging would be effective with Roselli, because Roselli stands only to gain from having the story of his CIA connection known and accepted. We cannot now suppress the story, because it is already out and may boil up afresh from the Garrison case. If we were to approach any of the participants and urge discretion upon him, and if this became known, it would merely lend credence to a tale that now sounds somewhat improbable.

SOURCES OF INFORMATION

Files were furnished for review by the Director of Security, the Deputy Director for Support, the General Counsel, the Legislative Counsel, the Chief of WH Division, and by Col. J.C. King, former Chief of WH Division. Biographic files and intelligence publications were furnished by the Director of Central Reference. He was not made witting of the reason for our interest in them, and those who assembled them for him were not told for whom they were intended.

We called back four officers for interviews: Richard Bissell, Sheffield Edwards from retirement, William Harvey from sick leave, and Nestor Sanchez from his post in ███████. Otherwise, our interviews were confined to officers assigned to the headquarters installation. We opened each interview by referring to the Drew Pearson column of 7 March 1967, citing that as the reason for our interest in learning of plots to assassinate Castro. We told those interviewed that we were on a fact-finding mission on behalf of the Director, and that this was not the usual sort of Inspector General investigation. We asked each to name any others who were likely to have knowledge of such plots. We cautioned each not to discuss the subject of the interview with anyone else — even others whom we might interview. This is a complete list of those interviewed:

Desmond FitzGerald
Samuel Halpern
███████

J.C. King
Alfonso Rodriguez
J.D. Esterline
Edward Gunn
Howard Osborn
James O'Connell
Sidney Gottlieb
Sheffield Edwards
Richard Bissell
Lawrence Houston
████████████

John Warner
Nestor Sanchez
William Harvey
Cornelius Roosevelt
Robert Bannerman

████████████
████████████

EXECUTIVE ACTION

634 Ways to Kill Fidel Castro

Fabián Escalante

CUBA'S FORMER HEAD OF COUNTERINTELLIGENCE REVIEWS FOUR DECADES OF PLOTS TO KILL FIDEL CASTRO

In a highly readable and informative style, Fabián Escalante reviews over 600 attempts to kill Fidel Castro. As Cuba's former counterintelligence chief, the author was responsible for countering the CIA's assassination project, code-named "Executive Action." Although melodramatic and at times quite comical, these plans were deadly serious—and illegal—as subsequent US government inquiries concluded.

This book is the basis of a new documentary about attempts to assassinate Fidel Castro, "634 Ways to Kill Fidel."

ISBN 978-1-920888-72-5 (paper)

Available in Spanish 978-1-920888-55-8

Published in The Secret War series

THE CUBA PROJECT

CIA Covert Operations Against Cuba 1959-62

Fabián Escalante

An intriguing tale of a "regime change" project that failed, this is the secret war the CIA lost. The "Cuba Project" included assassination plots, sabotage and terrorist activities, paramilitary invasion plans and bizarre psychological warfare schemes. This account reads almost like a crime novel, but as the former head of Cuban counterintelligence, Fabián Escalante was actually a key protagonist in this drama.

ISBN: 978-1-876175-99-3 (paper)

Published in The Secret War series

JFK: THE CUBA FILES

The Untold Story of the Plot to Kill Kennedy

Fabián Escalante

THE ENGAGING DECLASSIFIED REPORT OF CUBA'S INVESTIGATION INTO THE KENNEDY ASSASSINATION

Amid continuing speculation over Cuba's involvement in the most famous political crime of the 20th century, this book reveals for the first time the Cuban report into the Kennedy assassination. With compelling logic, Fabián Escalante, who directed Cuba's investigation, describes how Cuban intelligence uncovered a conspiracy against President Kennedy among those who felt betrayed by the Bay of Pigs debacle—the Cuban exiles, the Mafia, and the CIA.

Fabián Escalante is a former head of Cuban counterintelligence and a respected and sought-after authority by US researchers on CIA activities against Cuba.

ISBN 978-1-920888-14-5 (paper)

Available in Spanish 978-1-920888-07-7

Published in The Secret War series